IN SEARCH OF GANDHI

In Search of Gandhi

RICHARD ATTENBOROUGH

NEW CENTURY PUBLISHERS, INC.

ISBN 0–8329–0237–3
© Richard Attenborough 1982
Printed in Great Britain.

Published in the United States by
New Century Publishers, Inc.,
220 Old New Brunswick Road,
CN 1332, Piscataway, New Jersey 08854

The film *Gandhi* is dedicated to
Motilal Kothari
Earl Mountbatten of Burma, K.G.
and
Pandit Jawaharlal Nehru
without whose inspiration, unfailing advocacy
and faith it would not have been made.

Had there been no film, I would have had no
reason to write this book. I dedicate it
therefore to them and to everyone involved
in the making of *Gandhi*.

I carried 'Panditji'—as I eventually came to know him—home in my arms. It was about half past one in the morning. I'd just come back from a charity art auction at Christie's where each supporter present had either donated a work of art or undertaken to purchase one.

I had always wanted an Epstein. They weren't easy to obtain at the time. It was 1962. The sculptor had died only recently and the market was not yet flooded with his works, as was to happen eventually.

When I'd received the catalogue it simply said 'A Bust by Epstein'—no mention of the subject. I bid for it. I think, if my memory serves me right, I paid £220. The bust, cast in bronze, was of Pandit Jawaharlal Nehru, the first Prime Minister of India.

I had no idea whatsoever of the impact that name and everything surrounding him and his country would have on my life over the next twenty years. On arriving home, I put Panditji* on the table in the hall where he presided throughout what remained of the night.

At a quarter past eight the following morning when, I'm ashamed to say, I was still in bed, the telephone rang and a male voice enquired with the utmost politeness if I was Richard Attenborough.

'Yes,' I replied.

'Sir, my name is Motilal Kothari and I must see you.'

'But, Mr Kothari, it is rather early.'

'Yes,' he said, 'but this is a matter of great urgency.'

'But what is it about, Mr Kothari?'

'I cannot tell you over the telephone. It is regarding an undertaking of great confidentiality.'

So I said, 'Well, would you kindly ring my secretary in three-

* 'ji'—A suffix which in India is added to a person's name denoting both respect and affection.

7

quarters of an hour and I'll look in the diary and see what we can arrange.'

Mr Kothari rang back at precisely two minutes past nine and we agreed that I should lunch with him at Boulestin's Restaurant a few hundred yards from India House in the Aldwych a couple of days later.

That afternoon, Dennis O'Dell, a friend with whom I'd worked on a number of pictures, got in touch with me. He wanted to talk about my mysterious caller.

It transpired that for many years Mr Kothari had been a devotee of Mahatma Gandhi—as, indeed, had all his family who, in common with Gandhi, came from the state of Gujarat. When the Mahatma was assassinated, Motilal Kothari felt he could no longer remain in India. He felt that almost the reason for his very existence and certainly a major part of his life's work had been

Motilal Kothari in 1963 with his wife Dorothy, daughter Shanta and son Raj, who was born in England and worked on Gandhi *as an assistant editor.*

wiped out by Godse's* bullets. With his English school-teacher wife, Dorothy, and their baby daughter, Shanta, he decided—as was then his right—to live in London and joined the staff of the Indian High Commission.

Gradually, over a period of years following that terrible day in January 1948, Motilal Kothari came to realise that this decision was, in fact, a denial or—as he put it—a desertion of Gandhi and that somehow or another he had to make amends. He became determined to find a means of promoting the Mahatma's life and all he stood for; to make Gandhi's principles and attitudes known to the world at large. And what more effective way, he thought, than a motion picture?

He was introduced to Dennis O'Dell and, after a number of meetings, having tried unsuccessfully to interest one or two of the film industry's major directors, they decided that, at least by temperament, I might be a possibility.

I arrived for lunch and Mr Kothari was already waiting. He was very small, I would think not more than five feet, with the wide-jawed, almost moonlike face so typical of the Gujaratis. He was immensely gracious and greeted me with that most courteous of Hindu gestures, the *pranam*, placing his two hands together in front of his face. We sat down.

An early archive photograph of Mohandas K. Gandhi.

For some reason that I have never quite been able to understand and which, indeed, puzzles me even now, he felt that the whole matter had to be dealt with on an extraordinarily confidential level. I felt he kept wondering whether we might be overheard, whether those around were attempting to discover the topic of our conversation. In spite of this, he quietly told me much of his story and explained that nothing was going to prevent him from ensuring that this film was made.

He knew, of course, many of the figures surrounding Gandhi. He was not on intimate terms with the politicians such as Nehru, Patel, Kripalani or Maulana Azad, but did know a number of the English people involved—Horace Alexander, Madeleine Slade (Mirabehn) and Albert West who was Gandhi's first printer when he set up his original *ashram*† in South Africa during the early 1890s. He also knew Louis Fischer.

* Nathuram Godse: Gandhi's Hindu assassin who was hanged on 15 November 1949.

† *Ashram*: a self-sufficient rural commune.

In Southern Africa in the 1890s, a young Indian lawyer, Mohandas K. Gandhi (Ben Kingsley), is thrown off a train because, as a 'coloured', Europeans object to him travelling in a first class compartment even though he has a first class ticket. He is left stranded on a deserted platform and later described this incident as the watershed of his life.

Fischer was an American and a remarkably skilful biographer who had already written major works on Lenin, Hitler and Roosevelt. His study of Mohandas K. Gandhi was, and in my opinion still is, the best of all Western biographies about this extraordinary man.

I had to confess to Mr Kothari that I knew almost nothing about India—no more than a schoolboy's smattering of geography—and I knew even less about Mahatma Gandhi. What I did recall was the effect it had on people in Great Britain when we learned he had been assassinated. I was twenty-four at the time. The only comparable reaction came some fifteen years later, on learning of the assassination of President John F. Kennedy, when by a strange quirk of fate my wife Sheila and I were in Delhi. Like most people the world over I will always remember how, when and where I heard that devastating news. Gandhi's death had exactly the same impact on an earlier generation.

So Mr Kothari told me about Gandhi. He described the Mahatma's ideas and attitudes and his own hopes of spreading them throughout the world. I, in turn, tried to elicit why on earth Mr Kothari should want to involve *me*.

10

I had never directed a film. I had only in recent years become a producer. Certainly I was identified with a number of causes which could have led him to believe that ethically I might be drawn to such a project. But I had no reputation. Many eminent people had tried to mount this film; Pascal, Preminger, Michael Powell and, perhaps most important of all, David Lean. All had failed—or rather, at that particular time, none of them had brought it off.

Finally, over coffee, Mr Kothari asked if I would read the Fischer biography. 'Of course,' I said. 'I'd be delighted.' However, I went on to explain that until I had done so I couldn't possibly say whether, in the first instance, I felt capable of making such a movie and, in the second, whether I would have sufficient determination to surmount all the problems that undoubtedly would arise.

I had never wanted to be a director. I had been perfectly happy producing and acting whilst my partner, Bryan Forbes, wrote and directed. But naturally I would read the book, although time was a problem. I certainly could do so immediately after Christmas when I was due to go on holiday to Switzerland with Bryan and his wife Nanette, and my wife, Sheila. On our return, I would telephone Mr Kothari with my reaction.

A baffled and defiant Gandhi learns more about the indignities meted out to Indians in Southern Africa from a white lawyer called Baker (Richard Mayes). He can hardly believe that Khan (Amrish Puri), a wealthy Muslim trader, can employ Baker and yet not walk with him along the street. 'Well then,' Gandhi says, 'it must be fought.'

I remember walking back to the car in a sea of very mixed emotions. Here was something which could obviously alter the entire course of what I had thought to be my future career. This was by no means an ordinary film subject. It was clearly going to be daunting to mount financially. It would inevitably have to be conceived on an enormous scale. It was going to be very hard to script in terms of containing the story within a reasonable length. It was going to be tremendously difficult to cast and, of course, it involved going to India.

I wondered how I would react when I read the book. In a way, I felt inexplicably drawn to it already. Even without knowing any of the details, I was aware that Gandhi had spoken for the deprived and the dispossessed, that he was opposed to the concept of colonial conquest and that he believed unequivocally in the intrinsic rights of man. But whether Gandhi's story contained sufficient dramatic possibilities for a film was another matter. I was utterly ignorant as to where he was born, where he had lived or the kind of life he had led. I did know that he'd been assassinated, but that was all really, except for an awareness that if any one man could be said to have brought about the beginning of the end of the British Empire, it was Mahatma Gandhi.

I suppose, in truth, my attraction or the intuitive way in which I was reacting to this subject stemmed from my parents; known in the family as Mary and the Governor.

I adored them both, as did my two younger brothers, Dave and John, and, fortunately, as did all three of our wives. They were a remarkable couple. The Governor was nine years older than Mary and they were born, both of them, before the turn of the century.

Throughout my childhood I was conscious of their real awareness and resultant personal reaction to any situation involving the persecution of minorities or the denial of individual freedom.

At the age of eleven or twelve, the Spanish Civil War undoubtedly provided for me the first concrete and most dramatic example of their attitudes. Mary was Chairman of an area committee in England set up to care for evacuee Basque children. They came from Northern Spain where their families supported the left-wing government of the Spanish Republic and were violently opposed to the Falange, the Fascist party, headed by General Franco.

In Leicester, where the Governor was Principal of the University College, a friend of our family was a distinguished doctor

F·L·ATTENBOROUGH·M·A·
PRINCIPAL OF UNIVERSITY COLLEGE·LEICESTER·1932~51·

An engraving of my father by Malcolm Osborne,
commissioned by the College Council on the occasion of his retirement.

named Dick Ellis. He was one of a group of medical specialists sent to Spain to examine hundreds of these children before they could be evacuated to England. Mary set up this local committee which acquired and was responsible for the running of a huge mansion called Evington Hall. To that Hall there came sixty Basque children, ranging in age from, I suppose, about five to seventeen.

I remember I fell passionately in love with a dark-haired girl, who always wore a flower behind her ear, called Rosa. I used to cycle out to the Hall, perhaps three evenings a week and most weekends, partly I have to admit to see Rosa, but partly I now suspect because I was drawn to the drama and the extraordinary circumstances that had brought about this little community suddenly deposited in an alien environment. Through them I came to know of the cruelties and personal tragedies of war. I knew that Mary and the Governor felt unquestionably that in order to enjoy living to the full, you simply had to be conscious of others and their quality of life. It followed that you should be prepared to make some sort of sacrifice—and I don't mean that in an over-moral sense—wherever it was possible to be of help.

Gandhi organises a protest against discriminatory legislation by publicly burning the passes which he and his fellow Indians are obliged to carry at all times. Although beaten almost senseless by a police sergeant, the young lawyer offers no resistance.

But it was no more, I suppose, than the circumstance at home for as far back as I can remember, even in the late Twenties and early Thirties. I recall so well the impoverished areas of 'working class' estates around Leicester. We would go out there in the car, a great cream and brown Humber, a thing like a tank, which Mary drove quite well and the Governor drove appallingly. I think practically the only rows I ever heard between them were over who would take the wheel and who'd driven least well.

During the school holidays we used to go out to these estates with the clothes, particularly shoes, which Dave and John and I had outgrown. We would simply dole them out from door to door at houses where there were kids running around in bare feet. I remember it very clearly. It may seem hard to believe, now in the 1980s, but fifty years ago during the Depression there were families who literally couldn't afford shoes for their children.

In the summer, we used to go on holiday to Wales, to Penman Point. My brother David, three years my junior, used to disappear almost before the bags were in the hall, armed with a fishing net and a horrid little jam jar in search of sea creatures stranded on the rocky beaches. North Wales was also an excellent

Ben Kingsley as Gandhi in Southern Africa in the 1890s.

Gandhi with his wife Kasturba (Rohini Hattangady) and one of their sons in Southern Africa after his first brush with the law.

source of fossils, which he collected by the ton. How he didn't dislocate his back, I don't know, considering the amount he used to cart back to Leicester. Even at that time we were all beginning to see what the future held for him.

But when we went on these holidays, it was never just Mary, the Governor and we three boys. We were always accompanied by another boy who came from the estates where we made our forays with the shoes. And, for the duration of the summer, he became a member of the family.

However, having taken my leave of Mr Kothari and on my way back to the car, there was no doubt in my mind that the culminating experience through which my parents instilled a sense of social awareness came with the advent of the Second World War.

The Spanish Civil War had begun in 1936 when the word Communism had very different connotations from those we associate with it today. I remember our getting a brick through

My father's photograph of John, David and me on holiday in North Wales during the summer of 1935.

the front window because Mary had marched down the main street in Leicester, flanked by red flags bearing the hammer and sickle, with the leader of the local Communist Party, protesting against the terrible Italian dive-bombing of Guernica in Spain.

But at that time the full holocaust was still to come. How unaware we were, how ludicrously blinkered to its closeness as the brutal, barbaric regimes of Hitler in Germany and that buffoon Mussolini across the Alps ground relentlessly on. However, as they came more sharply into focus, it was inevitable that my parents would, must, involve themselves in the results of those frightening ideologies.

The Governor it was, this time, who chaired a committee to bring Jewish refugees out of Germany. Many of them were academics—brilliant scientists and research workers—and one or two came permanently to the College. The committee's main concern, though, was to bring Jewish children out of Hitler's Fatherland and get them to relatives in the safety of the United States and Canada. They would break their long journey in England to await the issue of the required visas. A number of our friends in Leicester housed these children for a week or a month, whatever time it took, until they had the necessary documentation to cross the Atlantic.

Frequently at home—we lived in a rambling old place with plenty of space—we would have, as guests, two, three, four refugees. (That sounds a familiar word now, sadly, but it was strange terminology in the late 1930s.)

Refugees—they were an unknown quantity, new in terms of what that word meant: huge movements of population, even nations, men, women and children fleeing, rootless, dispossessed, from varying forms of persecution.

One day Mary went up to London's St Pancras station to collect two girls, Helga and Irene Bejach. Helga, the younger, was covered in sores and Irene, who was eleven, had a terrible nervous facial twitch.

Dave, John and I didn't pay a great deal of attention. They were just two more German-Jewish children passing through the house. But then, with the declaration of war on 3 September 1939, everything changed.

If ever anything serious happened in the family, such as bad end-of-term reports or reprehensible conduct at school or the fact that I'd been nicking chocolates from the drawing-room cabinet, one was summoned to the Governor's study. On this

My mother photographed by my father.

particular autumn day when we got back from school, all three of us were told to go and see Father. Pondering our recent joint and several 'crimes', Dave, John and I climbed up the stairs to the first floor. When we went into the study Mary, somewhat unusually, was there as well.

They explained to us what had happened. Irene and Helga had left Berlin where their mother, who was Jewish, had been put into a concentration camp with their elder sister. Their father, who was the Medical Officer of Health for Berlin, was also likely to be interned because he was not prepared to make publicly the anti-Semitic statements the Nazis required of him.

Obviously it was hoped that eventually the entire family would be re-united. Meanwhile, the plan had been that Irene and Helga would go and live with their uncle in New York. But now that war had been officially declared, there were no more passages to America, even if there were visas available.

The Governor said therefore that, for the time being, Irene and Helga would become members of our family. They would, in fact, be our sisters. Because he and Mary didn't wish to usurp the position of their own parents, the girls would call them aunt and uncle. In all other respects, however, they were now as much their children as we were.

So, at the ages of sixteen, thirteen and ten, Dave, Johnny and I suddenly found ourselves with two little Jewish sisters. The Governor explained that what we had previously done as a family of five, we would now do as a family of seven. And if we couldn't do it as a family of seven, we wouldn't do it at all. There was to be absolutely no difference in their treatment of Irene and Helga from their treatment of the three of us. They were to join the family as equals.

This was, on looking back, a remarkable attitude, I feel, one of extraordinary compassion but utterly devoid of patronage or condescension. My parents made it seem the only possible way of behaving; perfectly normal and natural conduct. That particular decision, not merely paying lip service but taking positive, responsible action to help other human beings, made a profound impression on me. It has, I suppose, affected my life and my attitudes ever since.

Consequently, although I knew so little about Gandhi in 1962, the small store of knowledge which I did have after my lunch at Boulestin's seemed to touch a chord related to everything with which I had been imbued by Mary and the Governor. So the idea

Ian Charleson as Charlie Andrews urges his white congregation to consider the morality of the Pass Laws.

of reading Louis Fischer's book really did intrigue me. Although I felt extremely tentative in terms of committing myself to mounting a movie on Mahatma Gandhi, the subject matter already exerted a strong attraction. I felt the chances were he would prove to be quite a character!

Perhaps I should pause here to say something—in parenthesis, as it were—of my parents' background.

My father came from Stapleford in Nottinghamshire—not far from the village called Attenborough. His father was the village baker. Sadly, I never knew my paternal grandfather or grandmother, but my maternal grandfather is a very special figure in my memory and affections.

His name was Samuel Clegg, and he was a most handsome man with a beautifully trimmed Van Dyck beard, headmaster of one

Gandhi and Charlie Andrews (Ian Charleson) walk along a narrow South African street after their first meeting. Andrews, an Anglican missionary, was to become one of Gandhi's staunchest supporters and a lifelong friend.

19

*My father's portrait of
my maternal grandfather,
Samuel Clegg.*

of the first secondary schools in England, the author of a number of books about the appreciation of art and one of the gentlest, kindest, most sympathetic people I have ever encountered. My maternal grandmother was just a bundle of happiness; roly-poly, lovable and permanently abounding with joy. The first time I witnessed real grief was when my grandfather died. Both my parents were utterly distraught and my mother scarcely stopped weeping for three weeks.

My father owed an enormous amount to my maternal grandfather, indeed, the reason my second name is Samuel commemorates the love and devotion my parents bore him. One of my earliest memories is of sitting on his knee, I suppose at the age of six or seven, and his showing me a book of Canaletto paintings of Venice and telling me of this extraordinary city in Italy where people travelled by boats called gondolas — there were no streets, only waterways. I remember wanting desperately to go and see this incredible place which seemed so real and alive in those paintings.

Perhaps on that day, even at such an early age, my grandfather awakened in me an excitement for art: for painting, drawing and sculpture, which he had — years before — most certainly passed on to the Governor. I still greatly treasure two of the books my grandfather wrote and I often go back to them when I need to reassess the criteria one might bring to bear when attempting fully to understand and appreciate a great work of art.

The fact that my father eventually became the Principal of Leicester University College—retiring only at the point when, through his labours, it was about to become a university in its own right—was greatly due to Grandpapa.

Undoubtedly he saw an enormous potential in his pupil, young Frederick Attenborough, and encouraged him to take up an academic career. This resulted in the Governor going on from my grandfather's school to Bangor Teacher Training College in North Wales. There are some fascinating reports of his extra-curricular activities—not least of which was an evident aptitude for the theatre.

Having completed his training, he became a schoolmaster in Liverpool for a while after which he went on to Cambridge, having won a Foundation Scholarship to Emmanuel College, where he eventually became a don. In 1925, two years after I was born, he was appointed Principal of the Borough Road Training College in Isleworth, known now as the West London Institute of Higher Education.

Apart from his joy in art, the Governor's two recreational pleasures were music and football, the highpoint so far as soccer was concerned coming when he was selected for a trial as an England amateur. Cruelly, it was while playing in that match that he broke his leg which resulted, due to faulty setting, in one being permanently slightly shorter than the other. It was for this reason that he was rejected for service in the First World War.

Music played an enormous part in the entire Clegg household. My grandfather sang tenor, my mother (who was a most accomplished pianist) and her sisters soprano and contralto and my father baritone. There were frequent typical Edwardian evenings at Rye Hill Close, the Clegg family home, with the family grouped around the piano singing Schubert, Handel and—to everyone's great delight—Gilbert and Sullivan.

I have no doubt that my own pleasure in these very different forms of activity—art, music and football—derives enormously from my father's real knowledge of all three.

My first riveting experience of music publicly performed was in the De Montfort Hall, the big concert auditorium in Leicester, about half a mile from the University. The family went to hear the then Dr Malcolm Sargent, a local lad from Stamford, conduct Handel's *Messiah*. I recall my father explaining why it was that

ON FOLLOWING PAGE
Gandhi shows the American journalist, Walker (Martin Sheen), around the Phoenix Farm ashram *in Southern Africa.*

21

we all stood up when the 'Hallelujah Chorus' was sung and I equally well remember realising, when I sat down, that tears were streaming down my face.

As far as art was concerned, I recall the Governor taking me on a day trip to London with my brother David and my mother—Johnny being too young—to visit the National Gallery. I can hear now his uninhibited cry of joy: 'Oh, I say!' a shout almost, as he walked into one of the galleries to see Seurat's 'Bathers' hanging on the far wall.

As a result of those early, vivid experiences I suppose it isn't surprising that amongst my principal joys are my record collection of classical music, memories of appearing at a number of concerts with the late Sir Malcolm Sargent (who became one of Sheila's and my closest friends and our daughter Jane's godfather), my involvement with Chelsea Football Club and, ultimately, my appointment as a Trustee of the Tate Gallery.

The Governor was relatively small in height, Churchillian in stature though not in politics—both he and Mary were passionate supporters of the Labour Party almost from its inception. He was bald from an extremely early age, a characteristic I inherited from him. Indeed when I was twenty-four and playing the part of a fifteen-year-old schoolboy in the film *The Guinea Pig*, a small bald circle was already appearing on the crown of my head.

If the Governor wasn't tall, Mary was positively tiny. I don't think she can have been much more than 5′ 2″ in height, but a woman with more energy I've never met in my life. She was not unlike a film star idol of those days, young Jessie Matthews, a resemblance which gave my father a great deal of pleasure and amusement.

We lived very much, I suppose, in an Edwardian middle-class atmosphere. We were, as children, somewhat separate from our parents and influenced to no small degree by the nannies, few in number, who looked after us in the nursery. I particularly recall a wonderful Welsh girl, now Mrs Sims, and Nan, or to give her her proper name, Mona Pickles, a marvellous Yorkshire lass and a great favourite with us all. Nan was no mean cricketer and not only kept us in order with her tongue but also with the back of her hand when she thought appropriate.

I think my earliest memory of all as a child—even before that of sitting on my grandfather's knee—was being taken through the green baize door which separated our house from the Borough Road College. On the other side of that door, through

24

which, I might say, we were forbidden to pass under normal circumstances, was the Assembly Hall. I was taken through it on my sixth birthday to see, standing in splendid isolation, although wrapped in brown paper, what was unmistakably a rocking-horse, as beautiful a rocking-horse as I've seen in my life. Prince, I called him, why I haven't the remotest idea, but I did at once. He became an enormous favourite of mine, then of my brothers and subsequently of our children, and nothing would give me greater joy than to hand him on to a grandchild of my own.

In retrospect, I suppose somewhat superficial evidence of wanting to become a member of the theatrical profession, of living in my imagination, was evident quite early. I would spend

Looking at the score of Honegger's King David *with Sir Malcolm Sargent.*

hours riding Prince, galloping to some exciting rescue or fighting a major battle between cowboys and Indians in the then relatively unfamiliar Wild West. I am told that I indulged quite frequently in the creation of my own fantasy world. I had an imaginary girlfriend whose name was Jeannie. She was the cause of considerable trouble, for it was discovered ultimately that various packets of butter, sugar and dried fruit which had disappeared from the kitchen would reappear beneath the catmint at the end of the garden where I'd hidden them for Jeannie's delight.

Even at that age, I used to enjoy becoming part of a particular scene and I clearly recall spending a lot of time with a group of Cockney workmen who were digging up the road outside the

Gandhi leads striking miners to proclaim their rights as citizens of the British Empire. Mounted police charge the marchers to disperse them but Gandhi tells them to lie down in the belief that the horses cannot be made to trample his comrades. This proves to be so.

College. They were there for some weeks and my association with them had, as far as my parents were concerned, somewhat unfortunate results.

As I've said, we spent much of our time in the nursery, but always, including the occasions when there were distinguished guests for luncheon, we ate in the dining-room with the adults. It was a custom of the Governor and Mary, both in Isleworth and Leicester, to entertain people who were paying formal or informal visits to the colleges to perform or lecture.

I remember very clearly indeed meeting the great Czech leader, Jan Masaryk, a most kindly and benevolent creature who, in his broken English, totally won our hearts. Another guest was Sir Hugh Roberton, the founder-conductor of the Glasgow Orpheus Choir who introduced me to 'All in the April Evening', the most beautiful piece of choral singing I've ever heard. It was a recording often included in a classical music programme I used to

present in the 1960s for the BBC. Sir Thomas Beecham once came to lunch and made all of us laugh a great deal. There was Sir Stafford Cripps, Matheson Lang, the actor, and Mary Jarred, the marvellous contralto. She and my father used to swap somewhat crude Yorkshire stories—much to my mother's feigned embarrassment. We also met Eric Gill and Reynolds Stone, the engravers: it was Reynolds Stone who later designed all my company letterheads. Dilys Powell, the film critic, came to lecture and, oh, many, many more.

Anyway, on one of those occasions in Isleworth—I don't remember exactly which—around the time of my association with Alf and Harry, the two workmen outside the College, there was a pause in the conversation and I was heard to ask politely, 'I wonder if you'd mind passing the bleeding salt.'

My first formal appearance on a stage was as a fairy in *Iolanthe*. Later, as our dramatic society at the Wyggeston Grammar School in

Leicester annually performed one of the Gilbert and Sullivan operas, I was able to play Buttercup in *HMS Pinafore*. At the opening of the second act with a cello clasped firmly between my knees, I sang 'Silver'd is the Raven Hair . . .', a performance which, I fear, was somewhat more hilarious than touching.

By the outbreak of war in 1939, there was no doubt whatsoever in my own mind that I wanted to be an actor and, much to my father's chagrin, I spent far more time than was appropriate in the light of my scholastic achievements appearing in amateur performances, either at school or elsewhere.

First evidence that I might also harbour impresarial ambitions was my intention to put on a variety show at the St Barnabas Hall, for which I had to raise the formidable sum of ten shillings as the hire charge. I bought eighty little notepads for a penny, a similar number of pencils even more cheaply, attached each to the other with coloured string and resold the lot to my schoolfriends at threepence a time. All this was to allow me to appear in innumerable sketches. The problem was to find other members of the cast. One of the first recruits was Barry Letts, a schoolfriend of mine who today is a distinguished producer-director with BBC Television. Barry was a very willing participant. Much less forthcoming was my brother David. However, we reached a reasonable compromise. He would appear provided the hoped-for profits went to the Royal Society for the Prevention of Cruelty to Animals. So the deal was done and, for the only time in our lives, Dave and I appeared together in the same show; Dave in a blond wig, me in a red one—two charladies in a sketch entitled 'Ladies What Come to Oblige'.

By the time I was seventeen, things had reached a pretty pass at home and I really was not on very good terms with the Governor. He was greatly displeased with my lack of application as far as schoolwork was concerned and finally faced me—I think partly with my mother's connivance—with an ultimatum. He would apply to the Royal Academy of Dramatic Art to see if there was a scholarship available—since they certainly couldn't afford to pay for me. If there was and I won it, I could go to RADA. If not, I must undertake there and then to give up any thought of going into the theatre, at least until the end of my time at school and, possibly, even a period at university.

I think at the back of his decision was the fact that he had come from very humble beginnings and had himself gained such phenomenal benefits from a university education that he simply

An early photograph taken by my father.

couldn't bear the thought of any of his sons throwing away a similar opportunity.

Here, in later years, I do have to admit to a sadness at not having had the benefit of going to a university, as did both my brothers. But even if I had so chosen at the time, it would not have been possible for me to complete a course because the war was on and I had already signed up for the Royal Air Force Volunteer Reserve. So the chances were that any scholastic further education would have been peremptorily cut short in any event.

However, I accepted the Governor's ultimatum and therefore somehow or another, I had to reach an acting standard which might possibly give me the opportunity of going to RADA.

Mary was always a great ally in my wanting to become an actor. She was president for several years—and very actively so—of an exceptional amateur dramatic society, the Leicester Little Theatre. The society was run on professional lines and, apart from an early appearance in a concert party for the Ninth Leicester Cubs prior to joining the Scouts, much of my experience before enrolling as a drama student was at the Little Theatre. I owe it and a number of people still associated with it a great debt of gratitude.

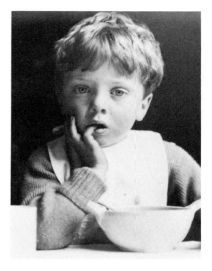

Photographed at the age of two by my father.

The director of the theatre, a wonderful woman named Moyra Haywood, coached me most patiently in my two 'set' pieces. One was de Stogumber's speech, having seen the Maid burnt at the stake in George Bernard Shaw's *Saint Joan*, and the other a truncation of the part of Ormonroyd, the tipsy photographer in J. B. Priestley's *When We Are Married*. I eventually went for the audition; my mama, bless her, accompanying me to London. We stayed at the Strand Palace Hotel. The night before my ordeal at Gower Street we went to see *Berkeley Square* at the Vaudeville Theatre with André Van Gyseghem and Jean Forbes-Robertson, with whom, some years later, I was to appear—my playing Sebastian to Jean's Viola in *Twelfth Night* at the Arts Theatre.

I presented myself at RADA amongst a number of other aspiring thespians to be greeted and comforted by two redoubtable ladies, Dora Sevening and Dorothy Saunders. When my turn came, I went down to what was then called the 'Little Theatre' to appear before Sir Kenneth Barnes, the Principal, Sir Felix Aylmer, Athene Seyler and Kathleen Nesbitt. Having somehow or another got through my two pieces, I retreated into the wings to be told by Miss Sevening that I would be informed by letter whether or not I had been successful.

Thousands of Indian immigrant labourers have been imprisoned in Southern Africa for peacefully defying the Pass Laws—among them Gandhi. As a result, the country's economy is in chaos.

I had applied for the Leverhulme Scholarship, the only competitive one the Academy offered annually. If I won, I would not have to pay the tuition fees which, at that time, were fifteen guineas per term and I would receive the princely living allowance of two pounds ten shillings a week during termtime.

Mama and I caught the afternoon train back to Leicester and, as we arrived, an air raid warning was sounding. I took her home and then set off on my bicycle to the local ARP centre where I was a messenger. I spent the night there and, at about eight o'clock the following morning, started out for home. As I was cycling towards the house, up through Victoria Park, two semi-demented brothers headed for me on their bikes, screaming at the top of their voices that I had won the scholarship. The letter, miraculously transported in those halcyon days by His Majesty's Post Office over a matter of hours, had arrived that morning to say the Leverhulme was mine.

When I arrived home, Mary was so thrilled she was in tears, and the Governor seemed absolutely to accept that this was the course I was going to follow. An objective endorsement, in the name of the Royal Academy of Dramatic Art, of the possibility of talent as far as I was concerned seemed to set his mind at rest and I have always had the sneaking feeling that, at the back of all his reservations, he really was quite intrigued at the prospect of a member of his family becoming an actor. From his early student days he had been a devotee of the theatre and used to attend performances at the Liverpool Playhouse. The cost then was a penny for a seat in the gallery.

When I was nine, I remember clearly him taking me to see Charlie Chaplin in *The Gold Rush*. He told me I would witness a genius in the relatively new medium of the cinema. He said he had never before seen a performer with this unique quality, an ability to make his audience both laugh and cry almost at the same instant, presenting 'the common man' battling against circumstances which often seemed beyond his control and yet managing to overcome them.

The Governor's deep commitment to his family and interest in everything they did was demonstrated at the end of my first RADA term. On my return home, I went into the study one day. He wasn't there but I noticed that his desk was piled high with books about classical theatre in Greece, in China and in Russia, contemporary American theatre and an up-to-date history of British theatre. Being an exceptional English scholar, his knowledge of Shakespeare was already both profound and adoring. But he also had this somewhat surprising interest in the cinema. The art of composition was obviously part of it, stemming from his highly informed love of painting, the rest came from his con-

On location with Ben Kingsley during the shooting of the scenes in General Smuts' Office.

Serving a sentence for peacefully defying the Pass Laws, Gandhi is taken, still in prison uniform, to see General Smuts (Athol Fugard), who informs him that due to the effectiveness of his campaign the laws are to be repealed.

David and me in drag for
Ladies What Come to Oblige,
1936.

*Scout Troup Leader
Attenborough R.S.
on messenger service for
the ARP.*

siderable talent as a photographer. He won the annual portrait
prize given by *The Amateur Photographer* magazine almost
every year he submitted an entry and captured members of the
family quite exquisitely, particularly Sheila and, of course, Mary.

The Governor had first met Mary when he attended a Suf-
fragette meeting. She was on the platform and, during her speech,
was somewhat rudely heckled by a man opposed to votes for
women. At the end of the evening, when Mary got off the
platform, the same man started to manhandle her. The Governor,
who was one of the gentlest people I have ever known, dealt with
the assailant as he thought fit and escorted Mama home.

They were, I think, the most perfectly married couple I have ever
encountered. They adored each other and, when Mama was killed
in a motor accident in 1961, the Governor was inconsolable and
hardly moved out of his room for over a year. He eventually died
nine years ago. I shall always be grateful to them for the example
they set me and, I'm sure, Dave and John as well, with love and
responsibility invariably shown to everyone around them.

The family home, if I choose one impression that overrides all
others, was continually full of laughter. There was always masses
going on—people coming and going—but essentially it was a
place of joy. The Governor was a marvellous raconteur and his
sense of humour and ability to communicate his own excitement
and involvement in everything around him has, I believe, stood
both Dave and me in very good stead.

My greatest regret is that, although the Governor knew something of my aspirations and plans for a film about Mahatma
Gandhi, Mary died before I ever read the Louis Fischer biography. I think she would have approved of the idea.

Together with the Forbes, Sheila and I left London Airport for Switzerland shortly after Christmas.

The four of us had been friends for almost ten years, although Forbsie and I had encountered each other some time prior to that. Indeed, we were even rivals on certain occasions for the same part in particular West End productions.

Our close friendship began, though, when, in 1955, Bryan was asked to write the screenplay for a film called *The Baby and the Battleship* which was produced by a marvellous swashbuckling character named Jay Lewis. Forbsie was to play in it and so was I, and the star of the movie was a close mutual friend, Johnny Mills.

The major location scenes were to be filmed in Italy and it so happened that Bryan and I flew out together, via Malta. It was our overnight stay in Valetta which earned me the nickname 'Bunter', one which has persisted ever since. It was bestowed on me by Forbsie, I might say, on the somewhat slim evidence that, having purchased six chocolate whipped cream walnuts whilst walking down the high street, I managed to consume all half dozen within fifty yards.

Forbsie wrote a splendid script for *The Baby and the Battleship*. His characters, as always, were absolutely real, founded, many of them, on his own observations. And, being an actor himself, his dialogue was always eminently speakable—a situation which was by no means the norm, even by the early Fifties.

From then on, the two of us and our wives were almost inseparable, but although our friendship flourished, one could scarcely say the same for our careers. Forbsie continued to write scripts in which he had no real faith and which, he felt, never reached the screen in the form he had intended. I, meanwhile, lumbered on playing in a number of films which, if I hadn't needed the money, I really ought to have declined.

So disillusioned were we with the possibility of achieving any work of a decent standard that ultimately, in 1958, we decided

An archive photograph of Gandhi and Kasturba shortly after their return to India from Southern Africa.

33

ARTY WELCOMES GANDHI

there was only one thing for it. We had to make our own movies.

We formed a company called Beaver Films, essentially to undertake a production called *The Angry Silence*. It would deal with a real social problem affecting people's working lives in Britain, an unheard-of proposition for a commercial movie at that time. The story was about a young factory hand being 'sent to

Coventry' by his workmates following a shop-floor dispute and an unofficial strike.

On a number of occasions following its production, Forbsie and I have been accused of being anti-trade union. Nothing could be further from the truth, certainly as far as I am concerned. I was a member of the council of my own trade union, Equity, for twenty-five years without a break. The sole reason for my resignation came with the formation of Capital Radio, the first commercial entertainment station licensed by the Independent Broadcasting Authority in Britain. As its Chairman, it was evident I could not be on both sides of the fence since I was bound to find myself involved in employer–employee negotiations.

The Angry Silence was not an attack on organised labour. It was an attack on the bully boys, on subversion and on the lunatic far left fringe of the trade union and the Labour movements. Until recently I was a member of the Labour Party for as long as I can remember, actively so since the 1945 election. I would, I am certain, have continued to be so had it not been for the cruelly inept and distressing decisions taken by the Labour Party Wembley Conference in 1981. To me, these seemed to deny many of the initial principles on which the whole Labour movement in our country was founded. As a result, I find myself far more in sympathy with the objectives and attitudes of the Social Democratic Party, of which I am now an active supporter.

Back in 1958 the subject matter of *The Angry Silence* caused even more difficulties in terms of raising funds than either Forbsie or I had suspected. He had, without doubt, written as good a screenplay as I have ever read but that didn't seem sufficient to prise a reasonable investment out of any of the major financing sources we approached. Finally, however, I went to see my movie mentors, the Boulting brothers, John and Roy.

They were, and are, a remarkable couple. Wonderfully outspoken, at times arrogant, hugely kind, generous, loyal, bursting with talent and a dedication to British films which has rarely been equalled. I first met John in 1943 when I was seconded from RAF Flying Training Command to the Royal Air Force Film Unit in order to play in a production called *Journey Together*, written by Terence Rattigan. John was the director and playing in it was one of my great heroes, Edward G. Robinson, and an enchantress, whom I shall adore for ever, Bessie Love.

When I was demobilised I signed a contract with John and Roy and played in a number of films for them, most particularly, I suppose, *The Guinea Pig*, which I have already mentioned, and Graham Greene's *Brighton Rock* in which I had played in the theatre before joining the Air Force. It was followed by the first of those satirical comedies which became very much part of the Boultings' trade mark: *Private's Progress* and *I'm All Right Jack*. I owe them an enormous debt. They believed in my ability to act

36

Ben Kingsley as Gandhi at the time of his return to India in 1915.

in movies and, indeed, actively looked for subjects in which I might appear.

John became a particularly close friend. There is little I have done in the forty-odd years I've been in the business that I haven't discussed with him, seeking his views and advice. I have to admit to not always accepting the words of wisdom that he offers, but nothing in all those years has impaired our friendship.

The Boultings read Bryan's screenplay for *The Angry Silence* and agreed to discuss it with the board of British Lion, which in addition to themselves consisted of Frank Launder and Sidney Gilliat, two extremely fine and individualistic British film makers, together with Arnold Goodman and Max Rayne, both subsequently created life peers.

Their deliberations resulted in a decision that they, too, sadly, felt the subject matter must mitigate against commercial viability. However, since they thought very highly of the screenplay, they offered to put up £100,000. Provided we could convince them that the film could be made within that figure, they were prepared formally to take it under their wing.

Forbsie and I therefore set about the task of trying to reduce the existing budget from approximately £140,000 to the required sum. This we realised finally was a destructive process. We were cutting integral sequences, reducing crowd scenes to a point where they became ineffectual, and taking short cuts which really weren't appropriate. The result was that finally, one day, I got on the telephone. 'Forbsie,' I said, 'there's only one way we're ever going to make this bloody film and make it properly. That is to take no money ourselves and persuade as many other people as we can to do the same thing. That way British Lion would be bound to give us a whacking percentage of the profits which we could share amongst everyone who agreed.'

The original idea for the film had been conceived by Michael Craig and his brother, Richard Gregson. We went to them first. They both agreed to forego their payment as the story originators and Michael, who was to play one of the leads, also agreed to appear for nothing. So did Pier Angeli, whom I'd come to know when we both appeared in a film which shall remain nameless, and Bernard Lee, whose face became so world-famous as 'M' in the Bond movies. Bernie, who sadly died in 1980, was a great pal of Bryan and myself, and there was never any chance of tension or depression on the set while Bernie was happily on call.

But obviously that was not enough. So we went to Berman's,

the theatrical costumiers, and asked them to service the film for nothing. That generous and kindly man, Monty Berman, immediately agreed. We went to the accountants and to the lawyers, each of whom also put in their services.

The result was that the film was made, not for £100,000 but for £92,000. It showed, and continues to show, a modest but very acceptable profit. Certainly everyone who participated in our gamble has received more than their original deferred salary.

The Angry Silence had marvellous reviews and did extraordinarily good business in the United Kingdom. But, most important of all, it established for the first time that the creative people —writers, actors and directors—in the British film industry were capable of making films themselves without the stultifying controls and punitive overheads that were almost always imposed by studios and major distributors.

Encouraged by this success, Forbsie and I went ahead with plans to make another film together. With *The Angry Silence* we had felt, and indeed were persuaded by British Lion, that we required a skilled and experienced director. We had engaged Guy Green and no small part of the happy outcome was due to his direction. However, on our next venture, it was inevitable that Forbsie should direct and I, therefore, would undertake the sole production responsibility.

At an elegant garden party organised in Gandhi's honour, Professor Gokhale (Shreeram Lagoo), the great Indian nationalist, extracts a promise from Gandhi that he will make no public speeches for a whole year until he has discovered the real India.

The film was *Whistle Down the Wind*, based on an enchanting original story by Johnny Mills's wife, Mary Hayley Bell, and we were able as a result of that, of course, to acquire the services of Miss Hayley Mills to play the lead. Again, we were able fortunately to engage Bernie Lee, who really was one of the most accomplished of British character actors. Together Forbsie and I raised the funds from the Rank Organisation, under the auspices of Allied Film Makers, a subsidiary distribution company we'd formed with Basil Dearden, Michael Relph, Guy Green and our great mutual friend, Jack Hawkins.

Allied's first production had been *The League of Gentlemen* in which Jack played the lead, and *Whistle Down the Wind* was to be the second. The screenplay was written by Willis Hall and Keith Waterhouse and we made the entire film on location in the little village of Worston, just outside Burnley in Lancashire. Although I say it, this was a beautiful film, exquisitely played by the entire cast and gloriously directed by Forbsie.

We made two other films together: *The L-Shaped Room*, starring Leslie Caron and Tom Bell, which Forbsie wrote and directed and I produced with Jimmy Woolf, and *Seance on a Wet Afternoon*, which I produced and played in and which Forbsie again wrote and directed. I think perhaps of all the work I've done in the cinema, that particular performance gave me most satisfaction—due in no small measure to playing opposite that remarkable American actress, Kim Stanley.

Forbsie and I haven't done anything else together since then.

It's far too long but, in a way, the separation was probably inevitable. Our paths began to diverge with the advent of a film which Bryan was to make called *King Rat*. I believed it should be shot *in situ* in the Far East setting but, ultimately, it was made in Hollywood. Mike Frankovitch and Columbia Pictures kindly invited me to produce it and to play one of the roles, but I felt that Hollywood was not a place where I could bring any particular production judgments and experience to bear. So Forbsie went his way and I went mine.

Ironically, after playing the RSM in *Guns at Batasi* in England, I too finally found myself in Hollywood playing in *The Flight of the Phoenix*, *The Sand Pebbles* and *Dr Dolittle*, while Forbsie remained in the United Kingdom writing, producing and directing a number of indigenous films including that superb piece of cinema *The Whisperers*, and eventually becoming Head of Film Production for EMI.

The fact that Bryan and I haven't worked together since the early Sixties has in no way impaired our relationship. No matter what the difficulties or the extent of the crises any of us may have to face, the Forbes will always be our closest friends and the love we share unstinting.

Together with Bryan and Nan, we landed at Zurich and took the train to St Moritz. By the time we arrived it was late at night

Bryan Forbes directing Hayley Mills in Whistle Down the Wind *in which Alan Bates began his now distinguished film career as 'the man'.*

and we were taken by taxi to the Hotel Suvretta Haus where we were to spend the next two weeks.

When I woke the following morning, the room seemed ablaze with light, even though the curtains were still drawn. Outside, the sun, reflected by an endless carpet of snow, produced an intensity of light that was almost blinding. It was bitterly cold and, although we wrapped up well for our first sleigh trip to see the ski slopes, the strong wind that swooped down from the mountains seemed to bite through every stitch of clothing. Back for lunch, a little rest and then off to do some looting. Forbsie seemed to purchase cameras and other photographic equipment at the same rate that we ordinary beings bought bars of Toblerone.

On our return to the hotel, there was a concerted dive for the English newspapers which had by now arrived and then a sumptuous dinner in the Suvretta Haus restaurant. The wealth and opulence on display in St Moritz was almost stifling—in direct

Indians travelling on the roof of a train hospitably invite Charlie to join them.

LEFT
Gandhi, Kasturba and Charlie embark on a series of train journeys that take them the length and breadth of India. On one journey their train is halted by a military engine ahead—derailed by Indian insurgents.

contrast to the last visit Sheila and I had made to Switzerland. That had been our first trip abroad together, just after the war, when we stayed in a little village called Rossinière which was very unsophisticated but gave us just as much pleasure.

Out again the following day, walking down to the village coffee shop, back for lunch and afterwards that copy of the Fischer book by my bedside seemed impossible to resist. I read the flyleaf notes about the author, I read the preface, and then there was nothing for it: the first chapter. It started with a description of Mahatma Gandhi's assassination.

I must admit to being totally enthralled from the word go. Books of semi-contemporary history or the historical novel have always been my favourite reading. Love stories and thrillers had never been for me, but books about anyone who has affected the world and our daily living hold permanent fascination.

The recounting of the Mahatma's funeral and his early life in

43

Filming action scenes with Ian Charleson on the roof of a speeding steam train on a stretch of narrow-gauge railway in the state of Rajasthan.

Gujarat, his adolescent education in England, his calling to the Bar, his return to India and his sojourn in South Africa captured my attention completely for an hour or more.

Then I read something which knocked me for six.

Gandhi was walking along the pavement in South Africa with a fellow Indian and two white South Africans were walking towards them. As was expected in those days, the early 1890s, the two Indians stepped into the gutter and the whites continued on the sidewalk. After they had passed, Gandhi turned to his companion and said, 'It has always been a mystery to me'—he wasn't angry, he was expressing surprise—'it has always been a mystery to me how men can feel themselves honoured by the humiliation of their fellow beings.'

I was thunderstruck by the extraordinary perception of this remark, made by a young Indian in South Africa at the age of twenty-two or twenty-three. And that was only on the forty-eighth page of a 505-page book. There was no doubt whatsoever that I was going to finish that book while my eyes remained open. The book was going to be a revelation. Through Fischer I was going to learn about a fellow human being who had shaken the

44

world with his advocacy and belief in *Satyagraha*, the name he gave non-violent passive resistance.

I don't remember whether I'd completely finished the book or not when I decided that I must try and telephone Mr Kothari in London. It wasn't easy, but eventually I got through.

He was delighted, no question, but he didn't seem surprised that I was so captivated by the biography. 'What about the film?' he asked.

'Well,' I replied, 'there's a great deal of thinking to do and, of course, it won't be easy.'

No, he said gravely, he had never thought it would be.

I explained that this would be a very large step for me to take and one that entailed enormous responsibilities. But that apart, for the first time in my life, I now wanted to direct a film, a specific film, a film about Mohandas K. Gandhi.

The next day I sent off a postcard to Mr Kothari's London home in Hampstead, just in case, in some strange way, he hadn't fully comprehended my excitement. During the latter part of the holiday, I read the book again and, as page succeeded page, I became impatient to get back to England. I wanted to discuss the whole subject further with Mr Kothari, to discover how far he had gone and to deliberate with him the initial moves and investigations which were prerequisites to any serious plans for embarking on such a monumental project.

I met him shortly after our return to London, delaying only for a day or so to seek the views of various colleagues and advisers on the viability of the idea. I have to admit that they were not greatly encouraging. Indeed, they voiced with some vehemence their considerable reservations about mounting such a film with its inevitable—even in those days—gargantuan budget. They echoed with some clarity many of the fears which had crowded into my own mind on examining the problems that had to be surmounted in order even to reach the starting blocks.

I had, of course, discussed the whole proposition at some length with Bryan, both in Switzerland and on our return. He felt that the problems of achieving a shootable script were huge. He did not believe, in practical terms, that it was possible to encompass some fifty, sixty or seventy years of a man's life within a reasonable screentime and end up with anything more than an unsatisfactory, superficial piece of work. In addition, he felt that writing about an essentially good man carried with it the awful connotation of boredom. What made drama was conflict, and

In a vast tent decorated with colourful pennants, a meeting of the Indian National Congress is in progress. The Muslim leader, Mohamed Ali Jinnah (Alyque Padamsee), demands that the British grant Home Rule.

inevitably evil, in some form, had to be shown in counterpoint to the principal figure, if that figure was one of integrity, even nobility.

In spite of these discussions, I did later ask Bryan if he would write the screenplay and I have always greatly regretted that, after considerable deliberation, he declined. I think he might have written an exceptional script, but to attempt to persuade him beyond a certain point would not only have been stupid but could, ultimately, have placed an intolerable strain upon our professional relationship.

I talked to my close friend and agent, John Redway, with whom I had been associated since 1957. He thought that to attempt a subject of this scale as a first-time directorial assignment was foolhardy, to say the least. He also believed that there was next to no chance of persuading any major distributor to finance such a film and the best I could achieve, at this juncture, might possibly be a relatively small sum from one of the British companies as pure-risk 'seed' money.

This opinion was echoed by another close friend, a director of several of my companies and our solicitor, Claude Fielding. He also expressed the view that if I was going to direct, I should attempt something on a more manageable scale before launching on anything with the inherent complications that shooting such a subject as this in India would entail.

The one person who advocated my pursuing the idea, without equivocation, was Sheila. Although it had never been mentioned aloud, I believe she always knew subconsciously that one day I would want to be a director. I had always loved telling stories. If I have any gift, beyond that of acting, it is an ability as a raconteur. Combine that with a tremendous urge to communicate—together with my fascination for visual imagery—then I suppose directing movies is where one should sensibly end up.

Despite all the reservations expressed from so many quarters, Sheila said that if this was something I really desperately cared about and was a story I was determined to tell, then I shouldn't let anything or anybody put me off. Needless to say, it was her advice that I finally heeded.

The fact remained that there were enormous problems and those voiced by my friends and colleagues were very real ones. I discussed them at some length and, I believe, in an objective fashion with Mr Kothari at our next meeting. He, however, was carried forward by an absolutely blinding faith. The film had to be made and made it would be, no matter what the obstacles.

There was nevertheless one particular aspect where his area of knowledge was very pertinent, since it did not involve the film industry but the reaction of the Indian Government to such a proposal. It went without saying that, unless we had their backing, there could be no film. National susceptibilities had to be borne in mind, the whole concept of portraying Mahatma Gandhi in a commercial film had to be examined in the light of Indian opinion. Right from the outset, it was obvious that unless we had not only the consent but also the active co-operation of the authorities there, both at national and state level, any thought of pursuing the idea would have to be abandoned.

Mr Kothari had a number of contacts in India within the Gandhian movement. He also had means of making contact with those in authority. The sole link that I could produce, it occurred to me, was my friendship with Earl Mountbatten of Burma.

When Gandhi is asked to speak to the National Congress he utters an impassioned plea for identification with the millions who toil each day under the hot sun. The speech is of such originality and force, it takes the members by storm.

Alyque Padamsee as the Muslim politician Mohamed Ali Jinnah.

47

Lord Louis, as we all knew him, having been the last Viceroy and the first Governor-General of the Republic of India, had become an intimate and close friend of Mahatma Gandhi and Pandit Nehru and his family. His voice would obviously carry more weight in deliberations taking place in New Delhi than that of anyone else alive.

I had known him ever since 1941 when, in my first professional engagement in the cinema, I appeared in the Noël Coward film *In Which We Serve* which was based on part of Lord Louis' wartime naval career.

There now occurred the second of the coincidences that surround the history of the making of *Gandhi*. The first had been my purchase of the Epstein bust of Pandit Nehru only hours before Mr Kothari made his initial telephone call. The second coincidence came on the day following this latest conversation with him.

I was at a committee lunch at the Mirabelle Restaurant, convened to plan the charity première of a film, *PT 109*, the story of John F. Kennedy's service in the American Navy. The event was to benefit the Variety Club and also the Save the Children Fund which, together with Youth Aliyah, had been one of the causes aided by that art auction at Christie's.

Noël Coward in In Which We Serve.

Amongst the other people at lunch was Admiral Ronnie Brockman, now Sir Ronald Brockman, who was then principal Staff Officer to Lord Louis. After coffee had been served, I mentioned to him that I wished to ask for an interview with Lord Mountbatten. What was I doing right now, he asked. I said I had no appointment for another couple of hours. He accordingly invited me to walk with him across St James's Park to the Ministry of Defence since he knew that Lord Louis had at least twenty minutes to spare before his first afternoon meeting. As we walked, I touched on the subject matter that I wished to discuss. Admiral Brockman made no observation whatsoever.

We arrived at the Ministry of Defence and, after a few moments of private discussion between him and Lord Louis, I was ushered into the great man's office.

As usual, he was immensely friendly and solicitous, asking in what way he could help me. I described my reading of the Gandhi biography. I told him of my discussions with various colleagues and I told him of my fears yet my determination to pursue the objective by every means possible until we reached a total impasse. I suggested that obviously the prerequisite of any hope of

Lord Louis Mountbatten on the set of In Which We Serve *with King George VI, Queen Elizabeth and Princess Margaret. Lady Louis stands behind the Queen.*

making the film would be the approval of India's Prime Minister and that most certainly there was no one who could more tellingly put the case to Mr Nehru than himself.

He asked if I would prepare him a short *aide-memoire*, listing the points I needed to put to the Prime Minister and, headed, naturally, by the most important question of all. Would such a proposal be one that was likely to gain Pandit Nehru's approval in principle?

I readily agreed to provide such a list within a couple of days. Lord Louis, displaying that marvellous sense of humour he possessed, suggested that might be a little late since, within a day or so, he was leaving for New Delhi to spend a week with the Prime Minister. It seemed almost too good to be true.

He told me that once he had discussed the matter with Pandit Nehru, he would communicate with Admiral Brockman and let me know through him what the Prime Minister's reaction might be. Needless to say, he was as good as his word.

Lord Louis had always been a great hero of mine on almost every level, ever since Noël Coward first introduced me to him on the vast sound stage at Denham Studios where a replica of his ship, HMS *Kelly*, (known in the film as HMS *Torrin*) which was to be such an integral part of *In Which We Serve*, had been constructed. Noël had told Lord Louis that this was my first professional engagement in the cinema and that I was, in fact, still a student at the Royal Academy of Dramatic Art.

49

He explained that he had tested me, amongst a number of other
possible lads, and that he had given me the part of the youngest
member of the ship's company—the sailor who deserted his post.
What Noël did not explain was how I'd come to be given the test.

At RADA there was a director named Ronald Kerr who also
ran the Intimate Theatre at Palmer's Green where he was
presenting Eugene O'Neill's *Ah, Wilderness!* He wanted a boy to
appear as Richard and obtained permission from Sir Kenneth
Barnes, the Principal of RADA, for me to undertake the part
during the vacation. I was lucky enough to play opposite an
enchanting Irish actress, Peggy Cummins.

Peggy had an agent. He was actually the doyen of London
agents—certainly the most renowned. An American, his name
was Al Parker. Al had directed the majority of the Douglas
Fairbanks Senior movies in Hollywood and eventually came to
London to set up his own film and theatrical agency. He married
a distinguished actress, Margaret Johnston, who later became a
partner in the business and has carried it on since Al's death.

Al came to see *Ah, Wilderness!* and asked afterwards whether I
would like to become one of his clients. Well, for a young actor to
have Al Parker request to represent him was something very
special indeed. I talked to my father about it. I was only seventeen
and he had to give permission for me to sign with Al, since I was

still legally a minor. But sign I did and on completion of my time at RADA was offered an understudy part by H. M. Tennent in the Vivien Leigh presentation of *The Doctor's Dilemma* at the Haymarket. I was so thrilled, I didn't know whether I was coming or going.

Al, however, was totally against it. He said that under no circumstances must I accept, since I would languish in a dressing-room unseen until I received my call-up for the Air Force. He persuaded both me and my father that the correct thing to do was to turn it down. He was proved absolutely right because subsequent to leaving RADA I appeared in *Awake and Sing* at the Arts Theatre and then, after several more productions there, in *The Little Foxes* with Fay Compton. Finally I played the lead in Graham Greene's *Brighton Rock* with Hermione Baddeley and Dulcie Gray. The play was written by Frank Harvey. I remember I earned twelve pounds a week, increased to fifteen after the notices.

One of the first things Al did after he had taken me on as a client

Kasturba and two other members of the ashram *are washing the communal laundry when they are hailed by Shukla (Manohar Pitale).*

was to persuade Noël Coward to test me for *In Which We Serve*. And, as a result, I got the sort of break that every young actor dreams of.

One of my favourite Noël Coward stories dates from that time. The filming of *In Which We Serve* required the building of an enormous indoor tank at Denham Studios in order to shoot a Carley float adrift in the North Sea with various surviving members of the crew clinging to it. We were acting in this tank for two and a half weeks.

The temperature of the water was kept tepid. It couldn't be any warmer because some very unrealistic steam would become visible, rising from the freezing 'waves', which had a liberal coating of oil to denote the sunken destroyer. Around the tank were piles of sawdust to soak up any water and also the increasingly rancid diesel leaking from the tank.

Co-director, David Lean, talks to Noël Coward during the shooting of a scene in the tank built at Denham Studios. The camera operator is Guy Green, who later was to direct The Angry Silence.

We ordinary mortals, particularly towards the end, used to lower ourselves as gently as possible into the water, holding our noses for the loathsome mandatory dip of each head to acquire a sufficient coating of the filth that floated on the surface. The stench was something to be wondered at and consequently nobody relished this early-morning dip.

The Master, however, wouldn't dream of emulating our undignified and tentative entrances. Each day he stood on the edge of the tank, lifted his arms gracefully above his head and dived in. With a resounding belly flop.

On the very last day, re-surfacing with oil, sawdust and filth dripping from his distinguished profile, he announced with that wonderful clipped delivery of his, 'There's dysentery in every ripple.'

To gain such professional experience as working in *In Which We Serve* whilst still a student was an immense piece of good fortune.

From In Which We Serve.

I have many other happy memories of my time at RADA. The students mounted a fire-watching rota during the blitz which meant that a number slept in the building every night in order to try and deal with any incendiary bombs. High explosive, of course, one could do nothing about. But fire, hopefully, was another matter. So we took turns to patrol with our funny little buckets of sand and water and accompanying stirrup pumps. Shortly before the start of the summer term in 1941 the Academy was hit. The Vanburgh Theatre at the back, in Malet Street, was almost totally destroyed and the front part of the building in Gower Street was very badly damaged—to such an extent it seemed unlikely that term could begin.

However, about a dozen of us worked almost until we dropped, re-screwing on the doors, putting cardboard in gaping windows, cleaning up all the rubble and filth in the hope that the Council, due to meet two days before the start of term, might decide we should be allowed to continue our studies.

We all sat, awaiting the verdict, in the well of the Academy's staircase, snaking up on either side of the hall to the first-floor Council Room. They had been deliberating for what seemed hours when, finally, the door opened and out came a legendary figure. Unmistakable: plus fours, neat white hair, a white wispy beard, his legs crossing like knitting needles as he came dancing down the stairs.

'We're going to open, children. We're going to open!'

George Bernard Shaw. I shall never forget it as long as I live.

In fact one of the nicest moments I have had during my period as Chairman of the RADA Council has been to suggest that the Little Theatre—as we used to know it—be renamed 'The G.B.S.'

It was at RADA that I met Sheila. She says she first heard of me when enquiring about a terrible noise coming from the Little Theatre after classes where somebody was thumping a piano and singing at the top of his voice.

'Ah,' said another student, 'it's that funny Dickie Edinburgh.'

Little did anyone know that the only music I knew how to play were those first few bars of the National Anthem.

I was greatly in awe of Sheila Sim. She was a term or two ahead of me and was a fully fledged professional actress before I even left the Academy. Her initial major success came when Michael Powell cast her for the leading female role in *A Canterbury Tale* for which she received enormous acclaim. She played in a number

Gandhi and Kasturba listen sympathetically as the starving Shukla describes the destitution inflicted by British landlords on the tenant indigo farmers of his native province of Champaran.

Word of Gandhi's coming has spread in Champaran and as his train arrives at Motihari station a vast crowd has collected. Afraid his presence will cause an uprising, the British decide to arrest him on grounds of disturbing the peace.

Sheila and I were married in January 1945.

OPPOSITE
The first poster for the world's longest run.

of other films, some of them with me, but it was in the theatre that our careers really merged.

From the time we first met, we saw each other incessantly. We were very much in love and finally married on 22 January 1945 while I was still in the Air Force.

Our first joint success in the theatre was *To Dorothy A Son* which ran for some eighteen months. There is, however, no doubt whatsoever that, if we have any niche in theatrical history, it derives from the fact that we starred together at the start of the world's longest ever run in Agatha Christie's play, *The Mousetrap*, which, as I write, is about to achieve its thirtieth anniversary. We were both totally devoted to Agatha, who almost adopted us, and Sir Peter Saunders, under whose management the play was mounted, has become our closest and dearest friend in the theatre.

We have one son and two daughters; Michael was born in 1950, Jane in 1955 and Charlotte in 1959. It was after Lotte's birth that Sheila decided, at the height of her career, to retire and devote her love and energies to the children.

To my total delight, early in May 1963 I received a letter from Lord Louis assuring me of Pandit Nehru's approval in principle of the film.

There seemed, therefore, no reason to delay choosing a possible screenwriter. Johnny Redway had gone into partnership with two astute and well-connected literary agents, Richard Gregson (of *The Angry Silence*) and Gareth Wigan. So Mr Kothari and I discussed with them whom we might commission.

Initially there was no doubt in my mind whatsoever that my own first choice was someone with whom Mr Kothari had already had preliminary discussions before we met. This was Robert Bolt, the author of a previous epic biography, *Lawrence of Arabia*. He lived across Richmond Green from Sheila and me and we had several exploratory talks. Bob unfortunately had to decline—to a certain extent due to professional reasons but overwhelmingly for personal ones—and I reported this situation to the Redway office.

Richard Gregson then came up with an original idea. He suggested an Irish writer by the name of Gerald Hanley. The originality stemmed from the fact that he was by no means an established major screenwriter. On the other hand, Hanley had scripted his own novel *Gilligan's Last Elephant* and he had an

AMBASSADORS THEATRE, West St. Cambridge Circus, W.C.2

Sole Proprietors: Ambassadors Theatre Ltd.   Lessees: J. W. Pemberton & Co. Ltd.
Managing Directors: W. G. Curtis & H. J. Malden.
Licensed by the Lord Chamberlain to J. F. H. Jay.

Monday to Friday: 7.30   Saturday: 5.15 and 8.0   Tuesday: 2.30

Stalls: 15/-, 10/6, 8/6;   Dress Circle: 15/-, 10/6, 8/6, 5/6;   Pit (unreserved): 3/6.

BOX OFFICE
Temple Bar 1171

Peter Saunders presents

Richard Attenborough
(By arrangement with the Boulting Brothers)

Sheila Sim in
(By arrangement with the Boulting Brothers)

THE MOUSETRAP
by *Agatha Christie*

With

Jessica Spencer

Aubrey Dexter

Mignon O'Doherty

Allan McClelland

John Paul
and
Martin Miller

DIRECTED BY PETER COTES   *Décor by Roger Furse*

In the cells below the Motihari courthouse where he is awaiting trial, Gandhi faces the painful task of telling Charlie that their present partnership must end. 'I have to be sure—they have to be sure,' he explains, 'that what we do here can be done by Indians alone.'

evident sympathy for our kind of project. This was plain for all to see in his remarkable novel *The Consul at Sunset* which, fortunately, I had already read and which concerned the ethics of British control and occupancy of an African territory. He was also familiar with much of India, having spent a number of years there. We all, therefore, decided to make the move for Gerald Hanley. Accordingly, Mr Kothari and I flew to Dublin.

Gerry is well over six feet tall and wears a perpetual, beaming smile on a craggy face surmounted by a full head of curly greying hair. Everything about him bespeaks an Irishman and he walks with that marvellous optimistic bounce that is not dissimilar to the very characteristic gait of Sir John Gielgud.

We settled down at Gerry's chosen hostelry to pool our varying degrees of knowledge and examine the viability of the film we all had in mind.

Of one thing Gerry was certain. Gandhi's life contained, in his opinion, all the essential ingredients of drama. He felt convinced that it would be a daunting job of condensation. Nevertheless, he believed there was inherent in the juxtaposition of two nations, embodying their co-operation and their conflict through the various individuals making up the British administration and those who held such profound aspirations for Indian freedom, great potential for a very exciting and touching film.

He told us with equal conviction that he would have to do a vast amount of reading before he could even begin to outline the form a script might take. Obviously, he would read the Louis

Fischer book, and also Fischer's other work, *The Essential Gandhi*. He would certainly want to go through the massive *Mahatma*, written in eight volumes by Tendulkar, and an enormous number of further works, some published by the Navajivan Trust, others by the Government of India's Publications Division, in addition to books from various imprints all over the world. There were also Mahatma Gandhi's autobiographies, *Satyagraha in South Africa* and *My Experiments with Truth*.

Gerry suggested we should help him to assemble this bibliography in order that he could start work immediately. In this way by the time Mr Kothari and I returned from our intended visit to New Delhi we might be in a position to reach some firm conclusions regarding the screenplay.

We left him in Dublin and returned to London. Prior to our departure for India, there was one other matter we felt it

A threatening mob gathers outside the courthouse. The magistrate ultimately capitulates and releases Gandhi, since he refuses either to leave the province or post bail.

With Rohini Hattangady, who plays Gandhi's wife Kasturba.

appropriate to investigate. Moti—as he now was to me—had previously had discussions with Dennis van Thal, who was Sir Alec Guinness's agent. No firm views had been expressed by either of them but grounds had been established that would merit further talks. I, therefore, wrote to Alec and it was agreed that we should meet within the next few days.

Alec seemed to both Moti and me the only possible actor to play Mahatma Gandhi. Not only was he a screen actor of extraordinary brilliance, but he was the only star at that time who bore any physical resemblance to this distinctive figure.

On 16 April we met for a cup of tea at the Connaught Hotel. Alec, one has to admit, was reticent; in fact, he had grave doubts about even the possibility of a Western actor playing this great Indian at all. Furthermore, he felt that the amount of time required to prepare and play such a role successfully might well rule him out because of existing commitments. Alec had, I learned, previously discussed the question of portraying Gandhi with David Lean during an earlier attempt to set up the production.

However, we parted on the agreement that any decision must await a first draft screenplay and, only on reading that, might Alec feel capable of making an affirmative decision.

Following further correspondence with Lord Louis, I wrote to Pandit Nehru's private secretary, Mr S. P. Khanna, requesting him to thank the Prime Minister for his interest and asking if it would be convenient for me to come out to India with Moti during the week of 20 May. Within a few days I received a reply saying that the Prime Minister would be happy to see us both in Delhi on Sunday the 26th. Of course I replied immediately, saying we would fly out the previous day and greatly looked forward to the meeting.

Caught up with the excitement of my first trip to India, my elation took a severe blow only a couple of days before we were due to leave. Moti wasn't at all well and it was unlikely he would be able to accompany me.

It was only some years afterwards that I learned he had had quite a serious heart attack before ever we met, and one of the reasons he pressed forward so purposefully was his feeling that he was living on borrowed time. The illness he spoke of on the eve of our departure was, although I didn't know it then, a recurrence of this heart trouble. However, even though Moti was unable to come himself, he had arranged for his brother, Vala Kothari, to meet me at Delhi Airport and be my guide.

On the morning of 24 May, the day of my departure, I went to see Moti, to obtain his blessing as it were, and left with a feeling of sadness at three o'clock that afternoon.

The plane touched down in Delhi at 9.50 a.m. on 25 May. My own heart was pounding as I made my way from my seat to the exit. The light was blinding but my abiding memory is that of heat. I don't know what the temperature was, I suppose around the hundred mark, but it was as if someone had suddenly flung open the door of an enormous blast furnace.

I walked down the steps and across the tarmac to the terminal building. After the usual formalities, I was greeted by a figure which suddenly materialised out of a seething mass of humanity waiting beyond the Customs area. Although facially Vala was very like Moti, he was tall and broad, but the same courteous smile and the *pranam* identified him without question.

He wondered if, before going to the hotel, I might like to visit Gandhi's memorial, built at Rajghat on the spot where his body had been cremated. Such visits are customary for followers of the Mahatma on arrival in the capital city. Being susceptible to gestures which are symbolic and have a sense of theatre, I agreed at once and we piled into one of those unforgettably hair-raising Delhi Ambassador taxis.

The Samardhi—as it is called—is set by the river, at the end of a long paved walkway, flanked by lawns and then leading through a small arch. There, surrounded by grass and flowering trees, is a great slab of black marble. It is inscribed simply, '*He Ram*,' the two words Gandhi uttered with his dying breath.

The closest possible translation is 'O, God.'

Vala having instructed me to remove my shoes at the entrance, we purchased a little bunch of marigolds. These he and I placed on the marble.

To this day I still follow this custom whenever I go back to India and land in Delhi. It is now much more than a theatrical gesture on my part. It is, I hope, a conscious demonstration —small though it may be—of my dedication, and a semi-public statement of the phenomenal responsibility I feel in having undertaken this particular film.

3 The journey across Delhi to the Samardhi was my first sight of India. Having driven away from the bedlam of Palam Airport with its suppliant crowds of porters and taxi drivers, we were confronted by an almost deserted, parched and barren countryside. Today, of course, it is bisected by a modern highway, but twenty years ago the roads were somewhat less negotiable. Local farmers herding their flocks of sheep, goats and cattle were oblivious to the requirements of motor traffic, and little caravans of villagers moving from one place to another were all that one saw of the people, other than those attempting to scratch a living out of the unyielding earth. But everywhere one looked, brilliant colours assaulted the eyes.

At Jinnah's house Gandhi meets Vallabhbhai Sardar Patel (Saeed
Jaffrey) and the young Nehru (Roshan Seth) to discuss new British
laws which will deny Indians many basic civil liberties. Gandhi
proposes to call on the whole nation to observe a day of prayer and
fasting—thus paralysing the sub-continent with what amounts to a
total strike.

LEFT

To the irritation of Jinnah,
Gandhi prefers not to ride in the
chauffeur-driven limousine sent
to collect him from the station
and, accompanied by his great
friend and benefactor from
South African days Hermann
Kallenbach (Gunter Maria
Halmer), arrives at the Muslim
leader's house on foot.

The range of hues produced by the natural dyes used for the women's *saris* was so beautiful that I constantly wanted to halt the taxi in order not to miss something that must be unique. Of course it wasn't and, as I came to know India better, I realised such sights were an essential part of its perpetual beauty.

We reached the outskirts of New Delhi, driving through the diplomatic garden city with its manicured lawns and modern buildings, the flags of differing nations flying from the roof-tops. On, then, through the old city, seeing for myself evidence of the teeming multitudes which, as I had always imagined, crowded the Indian streets; everyone busily going somewhere, and browsing unconcernedly amongst them the slow, drowsy groups of buff-coloured cows. Whatever risk your driver might take—and we seemed to career from one near miss to another where human beings were concerned—the life of the cow was certainly sacred.

After we had placed our flowers on Gandhi's memorial, Vala took me to my hotel in the Janpath and saw me well cared for and ensconced in my room. He is an enchanting man, like an enormous St Bernard, self-effacing, always present whenever he might possibly be required but never for one moment intrusive.

My appointment with the Prime Minister was at 8.30 the following morning, Sunday 26 May. As arranged, I had telephoned Mr Khanna, his private secretary, on the day of my arrival in order to obtain the details.

Accompanied by Vala, I left the Imperial Hotel, driving, as we drew near our destination, along the Rajpath towards Rashtrapati Bhavan, which stands as an ever-present monument to the time of the Raj. Built by Sir Edwin Lutyens as the residence of the Viceroy, it ultimately became the home of the Governor-General and then finally the President's Palace.

The Prime Minister's office is in South Block, part of a whole great complex made up of Rashtrapati Bhavan and various major government offices together with the two houses of Lok Sabha itself, India's parliament.

We arrived at the entrance where we had to complete the normal security requirements of identifying ourselves and filling in forms. An aide then accompanied us up the great stone staircase to Mr Khanna's first-floor office.

It was already a hive of activity with people streaming in and out, bearing the various files and messages that testified to the multitude of activities surrounding the leader of one of the greatest nations in the world.

64

We were greeted most charmingly by Mr Khanna and, since we were some fifteen minutes early, asked to wait amongst a number of other people also seated in his office. Prior to our going in to see Mr Nehru, Mr Khanna had a confidential word. Would I please be conscious of the passage of time while I was with the Prime Minister, since his day was very tightly scheduled and it had only been possible to allocate me thirty minutes with him. Naturally, I agreed at once.

At precisely half-past eight, Vala and I were shown into the Prime Minister's office. Mr Nehru, who had been sitting behind a large desk, got to his feet and greeted us with the now increasingly familiar *pranam*, inviting us to sit opposite him.

Very often, when one is familiar with a famous figure by virtue of photographs or reportage, the actual person does not seem quite the same when you meet them for the first time. In this particular instance, my reaction was completely the opposite. Mr Nehru was exactly as I had expected; he was of medium height, dressed in his familiar jacket and trousers and his customary white cap. He had a most sweet face and gentle voice but my

Pandit Nehru and his daughter, Indira Gandhi, around the time of my first visit to India.

65

Roshan Seth plays the part of Pandit Jawaharlal Nehru.
Here he is seen at Teen Murti in Delhi among the
rose-beds that Nehru loved so well.

The Viceroy (John Mills) is hosting a glittering garden party in Delhi when an aide (Nigel Hawthorne) brings news that Gandhi's day of fasting has brought everything in India to a halt. He orders Gandhi's immediate arrest.

abiding memory is of his eyes—dark brown, compassionate, attentive, with the ability to convince you immediately that you had his absolute and entire attention.

He told us of his conversations with Lord Louis and repeated his feeling of pleasure at the possibility of a film on the life of Gandhiji—as he called him. He asked me how much I knew of him. I replied that I had read *Satyagraha in South Africa* and *My Experiments with Truth*, that I had dipped into *Mahatma*, the lengthy work by Tendulkar, and that I had also read the Louis Fischer book.

My impression was that he was not totally in favour of Fischer's biography. I was not quite sure why, although I believe, from subsequent conversations, it was Fischer's analysis of the Kashmiri problem* which he found unacceptable.

* The attempted annexation of Kashmir by Pakistan, which resulted in Nehru taking military action which he followed by an appeal to the United Nations.

He managed immediately to dispel any feeling of formality and encouraged me to talk freely about my enthusiasm and aspirations as far as the film was concerned. He was by no means reticent in condemning *Nine Hours to Rama*, the film, completed relatively recently in India, which purported to tell the events culminating in Gandhi's assassination. Fortunately, I had seen it and could voice my own anger at its evident distortion of truth. He enlarged on this particular theme in relation to our film. It was not the minutiae, the precise dates and times of events, which he felt were important. His concern was that the spirit and fundamental truth of Gandhiji's life should be apparent in all that we might attempt to convey.

He asked me to enumerate what I thought would be some of the highlights of the film. I mentioned several major dramatic moments in Gandhi's life. Immediately Panditji launched into personal reminiscences, illustrating their particular impact upon his own life and that of his contemporaries and, ultimately, on the whole future of India.

He seemed convinced that the film, by simply telling Gandhi's story, could communicate the incredible worth of this man to millions of people and, indeed, reminded me that Gandhiji himself, when asked about the message he wished to convey to the world, replied, 'My *life* is my message.'

I was bubbling over with excitement. We seemed to have been talking for five or six minutes when I glanced at my watch and, to my horror, it was nine o'clock. I started to make a move—'What is it, where are you going?' asked the Prime Minister.

An archive picture of Mahatma Gandhi and Pandit Nehru.

'Well, sir, it's nine o'clock.'

'Yes, yes, but we haven't finished,' he said. 'Do sit down.'

Eventually he got up from his desk and took out an album full of photographs. Each one recalled some historic incident or some unique private moment. I longed to have a tape recorder in order to secure for the future all these unique recollections that could give such magical life to a screenplay attempting to depict the personalities of these great men.

The Prime Minister and I were by now on our hands and knees poring over more and more photographs when there was a knock at the door. A secretary came in and, somewhat startled not to find the Prime Minister in his usual place, he rather embarrassedly handed him a note. Mr Nehru glanced at it without getting up. 'Yes, yes,' he said, 'yes, yes,' and the secretary left. We went on with our talk. Every moment seemed to reveal some new element which should be considered and adjudged when putting together the script.

I am not exactly certain how long I remained with the Prime Minister. I only know that it went well beyond my allotted time. 'I want you to meet a number of people here,' he said. 'You must also see some of our officials and, of course, you must meet my daughter.' He got up, went to the phone and rang what was obviously his home.

'I am sending the English actor and producer, Richard Attenborough, to see you. He's going to make a film about Bapu.'*

He enquired as to whether we had a car. I replied that we had and he said it should take us to his house, Teen Murti.

'My daughter will be delighted to see you and you must come and visit me again.' He opened the door to the outer office. I immediately suffered a dreadful pang of conscience as I saw Mr Khanna's kindly but plainly stricken face looking towards us.

By now the ante-room seemed like Piccadilly Circus with a positive multitude of people, all of whom had been kept waiting for their appointments with the Prime Minister.

Indira Gandhi† was in her middle forties with no sign, as yet, of

* Father—a term of affection used both by the multitudes and those close to him when referring to Gandhi.

† The Prime Minister's daughter married Feroze Gandhi, a Member of the Indian Parliament, but he died in 1960. She is not related to Mahatma Gandhi.

Gandhi's imprisonment results in widespread rioting. Nehru visits him in gaol and describes the unrest.

the now familiar white plume in her otherwise jet black hair. We met her in the long sitting-room on the ground floor which looked out on to the gardens at the back of the house with their beautiful rose-beds that were Panditji's pride and joy. She was a most elegant woman, moving with a perfect carriage and exquisitely dressed in a very simple *sari*. Although she, too, greeted me with the *pranam*, there was an unmistakable air of constraint. She was very, very shy. She asked me to sit beside her on one of the long low settees. The conversation was by no means as easy as it had been with her father, but nevertheless she too expressed not only her interest but her enthusiasm for the idea of a film. She obviously had a considerable knowledge of cinema, not merely Indian films but also of those coming from Britain and the United States of America.

She asked if I knew of the Indian director, Satyajit Ray. Needless to say, I was delighted to reply that I not only knew of him, but thought that *Pather Panchali* was probably one of the most exquisite pieces of cinema I had ever seen.

In reply to her questions I said that after seeing a number of other people in India, I would return home to begin work on a screenplay which I hoped to bring back towards the end of the year. After about half an hour, I suppose, Vala and I took our leave and returned to the hotel.

I was to learn during the afternoon that, true to his word, the Prime Minister had arranged for me to see several of his ministers and particularly Mr Gopal Reddy, the Minister of Information and Broadcasting, who, due to the short notice of the request, was good enough to see us at his home. He too echoed the enthusiasm shown by Mr Nehru and Mrs Gandhi and said that, on the supposition that the script was found acceptable, he was certain the government would grant me every possible co-operation.

After completing the meetings arranged for us and spending a magical morning at the Gandhi Museum, Vala and I left Delhi for Bombay.

Before my departure for India, Lord Louis had armed me with letters of introduction to a number of people. These included Gandhiji's principal secretary and biographer, Pyarelal Nayar, whom I was fortunate enough to see and who gave me great encouragement despite having certain personal reservations until he was able to see a script. Rajkumari Amrit Kaur, who had been Gandhiji's private secretary for the last fifteen years of his life, I was unable to meet, since she was in Geneva at that particular time. The third letter was addressed to Vijaya Lakshmi Pandit, Nehru's sister.

Mrs Pandit, who had been the Indian High Commissioner in London, was now the Governor of Maharashtra. Upon our arrival in Bombay I was greeted at the aeroplane by one of the Governor's messengers resplendent in full-dress uniform, who gave me a hand-written note from Her Excellency saying that she would be delighted to meet me that afternoon between four and

five. Once again there was evident and abounding enthusiasm for the project and an offer of all possible help and co-operation.

My trip to India was ridiculously brief. I had arrived on the Saturday and by the following Wednesday morning I was back in London. Without a shadow of doubt, however, those four days were as memorable as any in my life. There is no doubt either that the kindness shown to me by Mr Varde and Mr Paranjape, two of

With Kim Stanley in Seance on a Wet Afternoon.

the Kothari family's close friends, together with the ever-comforting kindness with which Vala cared for me, ensured the success and joy of my first visit to India.

The principal reason for the brevity of my trip was that, with many production problems still to be settled, we were due to start shooting *Seance on a Wet Afternoon* on Monday 17 June. I had, however, one remaining pleasure and that was meeting Dr Sushila Nayar, Pyarelal Nayar's sister. She had been first Minister of Health in the Nehru government and was Gandhiji's personal physician for the last few years of his life.

72

She was not surprised by Pyarelal's reservations in regard to the film. However, she felt certain that, if the script was faithful in its interpretation of Gandhiji's life, we would ultimately obtain her brother's blessing. I drove her to London Airport in order to spend an hour or two with her while she was waiting to greet the President of India, who was briefly stopping over at Heathrow on his way to New York. Dr Nayar also offered me every assistance and one of my regrets is that as a character she appears for only one short moment in the film.

During the week that followed, I wrote to the numerous people who had been so hospitable to me. At his request, I also enclosed with my letter to Panditji photographs of the Epstein bust I had purchased the year before. In his charming reply he reiterated his interest in our plans. 'As I have told you, we are enormously interested in the great project that you have undertaken to make a film on Gandhiji. You have yourself experienced the lively interest that many people here will take in it and I am sure they will all help you.'

Needless to say, immediately on my return I had gone over to see Moti who was much better and seemed back to his old self. He was jubilant to hear of the offers of co-operation that I had received from everyone I had met. I tried meticulously to fill in all the details of my visit since I knew how desperately disappointed he had been at being forced to stay behind. And I told him of the real affection I felt for his brother after such a short acquaintance.

Moti and I both considered it not unimportant that a degree of confidentiality should be maintained for as long as possible; firstly in order not to jeopardise the government's nominal approval and secondly since we had yet to set up a company under whose banner we would produce the film. However, despite all our precautions, on 20 June several papers in India carried a statement by Mr Gopal Reddy, Minister for Information and Broadcasting, that the government was discussing production of a film directed by me on the life of Gandhi.

This was unfortunate. It meant that all our preliminary negotiations were now spotlighted. Furthermore, the premature announcement obliged us, there and then, to demonstrate that we had substantial financial backing and more than mere ideas in regard to the script and possible casting. Patently, this was not yet so and it therefore became vital to secure some tangible form of financial security with which to proceed.

I decided to take the bull by the horns and go to see John

During the week I started shooting Seance, *a film I had made the previous year was premiered. This was* The Great Escape. *With me here are Gordon Jackson and Steve McQueen.*

ON FOLLOWING PAGE
In the city of Amritsar on 13 April 1919, General Dyer leads two companies of Indian troops to seal off a political meeting in the Jallianwala Bagh.

Davis — now Sir John Davis — the Chairman of the Rank Organisation — the most likely major film company, I thought, to back such a project in Britain.

Even if one is not on a quest for hard cash, visiting the Rank Organisation in South Street is a fairly daunting experience. The two opaque glass panelled nine-foot high doors are protected by thick black glossy painted bars. There is a brass door bell — polished every hour, one would think — which almost dares one to press it. However, with trembling hand I did.

After a few moments the door was opened by a conservatively uniformed commissionaire and I announced that I had an appointment with the Chairman. I paced up and down the black and white chessboard marble floor of the hall while a phone call was made to Mr Davis's secretary. After another few moments I was taken up the massive black marble staircase. It reminded me of 'Xanadu' in *Citizen Kane* and, when I was finally shown into the Chairman's office, I was even a little surprised to see John Davis there rather than Orson Welles.

Not totally surprised in a way, because John Davis is perhaps not dissimilar to a slimmer and even more sartorially dressed business mogul than Charles Foster Kane.

Prior to visiting him, I had discussed the project in principle with Earl St John, the Head of Production for the Rank Organisation. Moti and I had gone down to Pinewood Studios to meet both Earl and his Executive in Charge of Production, Michael Stanley-Evans. There's no doubt that Mike Stanley-Evans was immediately intrigued by the subject matter and saw in the material an extraordinary piece of drama. Earl, a six foot tall, florid, silver-haired American, was I think somewhat less convinced, but he too felt the subject was worth pursuing. Nevertheless, they both expressed the view that the scale of the picture and its unusual nature would necessitate the full approval of their Chairman and they felt that the best way of gaining his interest was for me to go and see him.

This was how I found myself facing JD — as he is known in the British film industry — with his beautifully cut pinstripe suit, sporting, as always, a very discreet dark red carnation in the button-hole of his left lapel.

Almost before I had sat down — JD doesn't bother a great deal with unnecessary formalities — he asked, 'Why on earth do you want to make a film about someone like Mahatma Gandhi? Most of the world,' he said, 'knows nothing about him at all and I don't believe they would really be very interested.'

It was not a very promising beginning, but then JD was not known as being the easiest of people to deal with. Many found him very tough indeed and certainly a number on the creative side of the industry felt that he was lacking in sympathy and understanding regarding the creative processes which precede the delivery of a finished film.

How on earth did I think one could economically shoot a picture in India? Who on earth could play the part? What possible appeal could there be for young cinema audiences? It was a subject based on a virtually unknown principal character from an alien country and with an image, if he had any, of an old man dressed in a sheet carrying a bean pole. And, to top it all, there would be no way of making such a film within a budget which could possibly be contemplated by a purely British company.

My heart sank, but I ploughed on. Who, I asked, amongst the ordinary cinema-going public had heard of Lawrence of Arabia, and that had shown itself to be an enormous success?

In conversation on the set with Pyarelal Nayar who in latter years was one of Gandhi's principal secretaries and is now his biographer.

General Dyer orders his troops
to open fire on the crowd.
1650 bullets are fired in less
than fifteen minutes, causing
1516 casualties.

'Yes,' he replied, 'but that had a young, romantic hero in the person of Peter O'Toole.' Surely there was no similarity between that figure and Mahatma Gandhi? And how much of this man's life did I believe it would be necessary to tell?

I replied that we might have to cover some fifty to sixty years, but, until a first draft script was completed, it was well nigh impossible to know.

'Well, what do you want then?'

Taking a deep breath, I said, 'Well, JD, what I require is sufficient money to engage a screen writer of real calibre.' I told him that I wanted Gerald Hanley to work on a first draft, to see whether it was possible to encompass Gandhi's life within an acceptable screen length. I added, somewhat unwisely, that I really did believe the philosophies and attitudes that Gandhi displayed towards his fellow beings ought to be known to the whole world.

'For God's sake,' he said, 'don't tell me you want to make a picture with a message. Remember Sam Goldwyn. "Messages are for Western Union."'

I knew I'd made a ghastly tactical error. The silence in the room seemed to last for an eternity.

Then JD said, 'Dickie . . . I don't think that Rank could possibly make it. I'm convinced it will be enormously expensive and I'm sure—and I must tell you this—that it has no box office potential whatsoever. However, I do see that we shan't really know what there is in terms of a screenplay until one is written. You have made a number of pictures for the Rank Organisation and you are very much part of the British film industry. It would, therefore, in my opinion, be pretty shabby if the Rank Organisation were not to give you a chance to explore this idea . . . How much money do you want?'

I paused for a beat, I think it was only a second or two, since I wasn't quite prepared for such a direct question. 'Oh,' I said airily, '£2,500 to £3,000—I think I could get a first draft for that.'

'Right,' he said, 'I will send you a cheque for £5,000. It will be a personal loan to you. If we should decide to go ahead with the film—which I very much doubt—then it becomes part of the budget. If you set up the film ultimately with another company, I will expect the money to be returned to us plus the appropriate interest. If, however, you fail to make the film, then that is that, and you are under no obligation to this company whatsoever.'

It gives me some satisfaction to record this story about JD since

I gather it might be thought somewhat exceptional. Furthermore, he never even mentioned my inexperience or the fact that I was basically an actor.

Two days later the cheque for £5,000 arrived. Without it, *Gandhi* would never have got off the ground.

At this juncture Moti felt it appropriate to tell me of certain negotiations which had taken place before we first met. He had had a number of discussions with possible rupee financiers who might be prepared to put up a proportion of the initial Indian expenditure even though they did not necessarily intend to back the production as a whole. They had agreed, under specified conditions, to supply at least the initial funding required and, now that we had some finance from the Rank Organisation and I personally had given an undertaking to supply further money, Moti decided to disclose the Indians' identity.

Consequently he arranged a dinner with the Maharaja of Baroda and his emissary, Bobby Kadam. Now Jackie Baroda is everything that you might expect when you are told you are about to meet an Indian Maharaja. He is, I suppose, about 5′ 6″ in height and if, by some magic wand, you brought to life the jolly emblem that identifies Air India on all its advertisements . . . that would be Jackie. He is a gloriously expansive character who seems to be incessantly in fits of laughter. He is immensely engaging, flamboyantly courteous, great fun to be with and, should you be interested in cricket, ready with an endless stream of anecdotes.

He has been deeply involved in Indian test cricket over many years. His annual social or business diary is always determined, year after year, by the particular tour that the Indian test players are undertaking.

There appeared to be no doubt in Jackie's mind that the film ought to be made. As to precisely what aspects of Gandhi's life

John Mills as the Viceroy.

should be emphasised, that was another matter, and he preferred, he said, to leave those decisions to the makers of the film. He would, however, wish to retain the right to express his views on the ultimate script and have those views properly considered.

Following our dinner, the contract was drawn up and forwarded to Jackie. I thought it a happy coincidence that this was the first use of our new company letterhead, designed by Reynolds Stone and printed by the Curwen Press, incorporating the recently registered name of Indo-British Films Limited. In the agreement, Jackie undertook to provide the rupee cost of our initial reconnaissance trip.

By now, I was deeply involved with both playing in and producing *Seance on a Wet Afternoon*. As I've said before, it was a

In the wake of the Amritsar massacre a conference is held in Delhi, chaired by the Viceroy. Gandhi informs him that he will lead the Indian nation in a policy of non-violent non-cooperation that will finally compel the British to leave.

part from which I derived enormous satisfaction and I also think it was as good a piece of screen acting as I have ever achieved.

It meant, of course, that my attention had to be divided between *Seance* and *Gandhi*. Obviously I had to go on working; I had to have an income since the money that had been made available from elsewhere was insufficient to cover both Gerry's contract, living expenses and so on and the sterling required for the forthcoming trip to India. Over the past few years Moti had spent a considerable sum and it now seemed only proper that I should put in roughly the same amount. There had already been my trip to India but many other items of expenditure also arose —lawyers, secretarial staff, cables, phone calls, together with the other paraphernalia that always accompanies the setting up of a film.

And so I would spend the day at the studios working on *Seance*—I had a long and complicated make-up, completely altering the shape of my profile and requiring a call at something like 6.30 each morning. At 7.00 or 7.30 at night I would join Gerry Hanley in talking through what form and shape the *Gandhi* screenplay should take, how we should begin, and where to place the main emphases in this extraordinary and varied life we were attempting to tell in terms of cinema.

Kasturba, three of her sons and a nephew. An archive photograph taken in South Africa.

Gerry Hanley's scholarship was very considerable. Moti and I had only discussed our project in outline with him at the beginning of May and yet, three months later, here he was in England, with a depth of knowledge that was quite remarkable. Twentieth-century history interested him immensely and he was fully conversant with the shifting balances and attitudes that had brought about each succeeding power structure in the modern world. But, in addition, he had that ability given to certain people to read reams of material—much of it documentary in form—and bank this store of information in some recess of his mind, upon which he could call at a moment's notice. One advantage was that he was able to set Gandhiji's life in the context of global events. Although it didn't necessarily mean that one took advantage of this information in the construction of the script directly, one was aware of the other forces existing contemporaneously with Gandhi's own impact on India, and throughout the rest of the world.

I had by now completed shooting on *Seance on a Wet Afternoon* and, although it had required an enormous amount of concentration, even during the filming I had devoted any spare moments to the library that I was accumulating on the Mahatma. Consequently, I was beginning to piece together the principal circumstances which made up his life.

Mohandas Karamchand Gandhi was born on 2 October 1869 in Porbandar, in the State of Gujarat. Devoted to both his parents, he was devastated by the death of his father when he himself was only in his teens, an event made even more traumatic by virtue of his being in bed with his young wife when he should have been tending his father. Through the Indian custom of arranged marriages, at the age of thirteen he had wed Kasturba Makanji. He was a passionate young man, and his desire for Kasturba knew no bounds. He was jealous of her attention, and demanded her subservience to his every wish.

He was, of course, a Hindu, and his family sect the Pranami.

At an open air rally, Gandhi urges his followers to remove untouchability from their hearts and minds and to practise Hindu-Muslim unity.

In his endeavours to alleviate poverty by fostering village crafts such as weaving, Gandhi exhorts Indians to burn all imported cloth and, like him, wear only homespun.

Gandhi with Mohamed Ali Jinnah, the Muslim leader, September 1944. An archive photograph.

This meant that he was a vegetarian, a conviction that he adhered to all his life, with the one exception of a short and distressing episode when he was persuaded to eat goat's meat by a school friend. He recalled that, having eaten it, for days he felt he could hear the goat bleating in his stomach. His academic achievements were not particularly distinguished. Nevertheless, he was by no means a fool. He wanted to become a lawyer and, despite opposition from the elders of his family, eventually in 1888 he left for London, where he was to study for the Bar.

He stayed in England for approximately two years, during the early part of which he attempted to become a totally accepted, Westernised, English gentleman. He wore a frock coat with a high wing collar, carried a silk top hat and a silver-topped cane, and sported a gold watch chain. He took dancing and violin lessons and wore grey gloves and spats. However, being the person that he was, he soon realised that there was something ridiculous in these activities and, in any event, his funds were now running low. He had to move from one set of lodgings to another, each more humble than the last. He was very lonely in London, although he recalled always the kindness he was shown by those with whom he came in contact. I feel certain that the impression English people made upon him in those formative years greatly affected his attitude when he became such an influential figure in India's relationship with the British in the first half of the twentieth century. In his writings, he recalls vividly his first sight of a butcher's shop, with the carcasses hanging in the window. It made him physically ill, and he nearly fainted. The one aspect of his leisure time in London which was truly enjoyable was his association with the Vegetarian Society, of which he became Secretary, a fact that would have enormously pleased his mother, since he had sworn an oath to her that he would 'not touch wine, women or meat' whilst abroad.

He was called to the Bar and enrolled in the High Court, returning to India on the SS *Assam* in 1891. During his absence two major events had occurred within his family. His mother, whom he adored, had died; and Kasturba had given birth to their first son, whom they named Harilal. Work appeared to be almost non-existent in the State of Gujarat; he tried Bombay, unsuccessfully. There then occurred the most extraordinary piece of good fortune, an event which had profound repercussions, not only on his own life, but on the lives of millions of others, particularly the Indian nation. A family friend required a lawyer to follow through a routine case in Southern Africa. Young Gandhi was engaged by Abdulla Sheth to sail to Durban and then travel overland to Pretoria in order to undertake the assignment. He left India in 1893 and arrived on the continent of Africa in May. On his way to Pretoria by train, the possessor of a first-class ticket purchased for him by Abdulla Sheth, he was suddenly confronted by a European and the conductor of the train, demanding

An archive photograph of Gandhi with Maulana Azad, his great Muslim friend and political colleague.

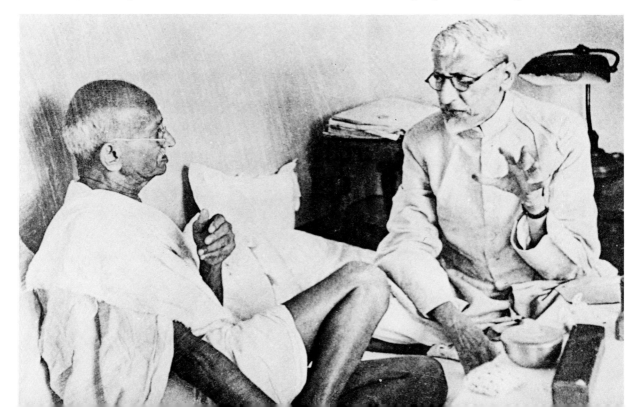

In middle age, Gandhi determines that Kasturba will teach him to use a spinning-wheel. She finds his initial clumsiness vastly amusing but, once he has mastered this craft, Gandhi will practise it every day for the rest of his life.

to know why he was occupying a first-class carriage. He produced his ticket but to no avail. They ordered him out. As a result of his refusal to leave the carriage, he was finally thrown off the train at Pietermaritzburg. Freezing cold, he spent the night sitting on the platform. He simply could not believe that, merely because of the colour of his skin, there could be people who would object to his travelling in a first-class carriage. He was devastated—in fact, he referred to this event as the watershed of his life. The result was that he decided with a number of friends, both Indian and English, that something had to be done regarding the whole question of the rights of the indentured labourers from India who were treated so appallingly. He masterminded a series of protests and then resultant negotiations in an attempt to bring about a decent way of life for those who had left their own country and were attempting, either temporarily or permanently, to set up home in Africa.

Over a period of years, he made several trips back to India, one to collect Kasturba and his two sons, and another during which he talked passionately of the indignities and cruelties which were heaped upon Indians in Southern Africa.

Although having great sympathy for those opposed to the British during the Boer War and the Zulu Rebellion, Gandhi felt that if Indians were to attain equality and claim the benefits of British citizenship, they must also accept the incumbent responsibilities. He therefore formed volunteer ambulance corps, whose bravery tending the wounded in battle cost many Indian lives.

It was in Africa that he first began to experiment with his ideas of the simple life, influenced not only by reading Ruskin's *Unto This Last* but also by his own inherent beliefs, and it was here that he first set up his *ashrams*, his kibbutzes, his communal farms, whatever one chooses to call them. There were two in Africa, Phoenix Farm and Tolstoy Farm, the latter named after his great hero. He also met a number of people who became lifelong friends: Charlie Andrews, the clergyman who became his closest English friend, and Hermann Kallenbach, the Jewish benefactor who, through his generosity, made the second *ashram* possible.

Kasturba found this new way of life very difficult to accept. In the first place, she had been brought up with a strict adherence to the Hindu caste system, involving inevitably the use of Untouchables in the household to do all the unpalatable work. Gandhiji not only brought Untouchables into the farm to live as

Amongst those, from all over the world, who are drawn to Gandhi's cause, is the daughter of an English admiral. Her name is Madeleine Slade but, from the moment of her arrival at the Sabarmati ashram, *she is known only as Mirabehn, the name conferred on her by the Mahatma. Mirabehn is played by Geraldine James.*

equals, but himself took on, as part of the routine living of the *ashram*, a number of the tasks which, under normal circumstances, would have been left solely to the Untouchables.

His assimilation of this lowest of all Hindu castes into his own community caused Gandhi untold difficulties throughout his life, but his conviction was unshakeable and indeed he ultimately named them Harijans (Children of God). This particular question was by no means the only one that caused dissension between Gandhiji and Kasturba. He was eminently successful in his profession, and in fact became a very wealthy man. Gifts were heaped upon him by the rich merchants who benefited from his legal skills, but he believed that in order to discover the *truth* he must rid himself of all earthly possessions. Consequently, he decided either to give away or sell, for the support of the *ashram*, not only his own possessions, but Kasturba's as well, including a considerable amount of jewellery. This Kasturba was determined to retain, not necessarily for her own pleasure, but in order to pass it on to any future daughters-in-law. She was virtually an illiterate, which infuriated Gandhi, and he was perpetually taunting her and attempting to teach her to read and write.

However, perhaps the most far-reaching agreement they achieved during these years was the vow of *brahmacharya*, taken when both were thirty-seven. Gandhiji had slowly come to the personal realisation that, in order to create absolute peace within himself and gain the ability to react with love and compassion to all peoples and all circumstances, he must rid himself of physical desires. *Brahmacharya* means the cessation of all sexual activity; this decision they arrived at together. It appears in no way to have eroded their remarkable relationship, and who is to say that in fact, as the years passed, it did not enhance it.

Inevitably, he came into contact with Jan Christian Smuts, who was the Minister in charge of Asiatic affairs. Both men, although eventually achieving not only great respect but indeed affection for each other, bargained very hard. Ultimately, there is no question that Gandhi was the victor in establishing civil rights for the Indian population.

It is amazing when one realises that Gandhiji spent over twenty years in Africa and did not return to India to take up his great crusade for Indian independence until he was forty-five. He landed in Bombay in January 1915. He had travelled via Europe, attempting whilst in London once again to raise an Indian ambulance corps to serve in the First World War. This time, however, he was unsuccessful. The fame he had achieved during his campaigning in Africa preceded him to India. He was lionised and met in the first few months of his return a number of the major figures who were, or would soon be, involved in the formation of the Congress Party—Lokamanya Tilak, Annie Besant, Lala Lajpat Rai, Vallabhbhai (Sardar) Patel, and Mohamed Ali Jinnah. His principal mentor, who sadly died within a year of his return, was the great Indian patriot, Professor Gokhale. Gokhale persuaded him that, before making any major pronouncements in India, he should familiarise himself with the sub-continent and its people, and he extracted a promise that Gandhiji would in fact make no public utterances for at least twelve months.

The initial major social campaign in which Gandhiji was involved was that of the Bihar indigo farmers' protests in Champaran. Unquestionably, this particular campaign, which occupied several years of his life, established him as a major national figure. He confronted British authority, always to the fullest extent, making overt use of the law. He won a very sizeable victory, for the British authorities were forced to take action as a result of the voluminous evidence he finally amassed to back up his case. There was a rebate of rents paid and the farmers were allowed at last to grow and sell crops of their own choosing.

Gandhi with his devoted follower, Mirabehn, the daughter of an English admiral. An archive photograph.

At the first National Congress Conference Gandhi attended he was content merely to act as a party worker, satisfying himself by sticking stamps on circulars. However, at the Lahore Conference in 1917, with a speech of such originality and force it took the members by storm, he established himself not only as a prominent figure within the Congress Party, but as one committed to achieving India's independence.

The first important move towards this end was his declaration of a national day of prayer and fasting on 6 April 1919, a national strike in other words, as perhaps the realists would describe the event. It was a demonstration covering the whole country in order to focus attention on the cause and it was completely successful. It brought India to a standstill, and Gandhiji, not for the first time, was put in prison.

It was only a few days later that the most cataclysmic event of all took place in the north-west of India in the holy city of the Sikhs, Amritsar. General Dyer ordered Indian troops to fire upon a crowd of 15,000 Indians attending a public meeting in the Jallianwala Bagh, resulting in 379 killed and 1,137 injured—men, women and children. It is true that, on his appointment as com-

93

manding officer of the troops in that district, the general had issued an order that there should be no public meetings. It is true that this meeting was held in defiance of that order, although it is questionable as to whether the majority of those gathered in the Bagh were aware of the proclamation. The fact remains that in this enclosed area the casualties were dreadful and there is little doubt that this particular event presaged the demise of the British occupation of India: indeed, it probably heralded the beginning of the end of what we know as the British Empire.

General Dyer was not dismissed, but he was relieved of his command as a result of the findings of the Hunter Commission. He returned to England, where a considerable portion of the populace greeted him as a hero. The House of Lords passed a vote of thanks, acknowledging his 'patriotism' and a national newspaper was responsible for raising some £20,000 which was handed over to him together with a silver sword with a laudatory inscription. The more responsible elements were of course appalled by the brutality of Dyer's actions, and so, one must say, was His Majesty's Government. Gandhi and his fellow Congress leaders told Britain that there was no alternative now—they must leave. In September 1920, Congress embarked upon a policy of peaceful, non-violent non-cooperation. Up and down the country, Indians refused any involvement in administration, in commerce, and in the process of law. Eminent public figures such as Motilal Nehru, Pandit Nehru's father, committed themselves to the Congress movement.

There followed a short time later the tragedy of Chauri Chaura. Obviously, whenever a form of protest is unleashed, however peaceful its intentions may be, there always remains the risk of possible violence, and this in fact occurred. What started as a peaceful protest resulted in the massacre of twenty-two Indian policemen by a mob who, having set the police station on fire, hacked the policemen to pieces as they emerged from the burning building.

Gandhiji was profoundly shocked, and in despair. He demanded from his fellow Congressmen the cessation of all protest activity and the end of non-cooperation with British authority. He was resisted vigorously, not only by a number of the leaders but by many of the party workers throughout the country, and Gandhiji resorted to a device which he used on a number of occasions during his life—that of fasting. He undertook a fast unto death until all co-operation with the British was restored

At Chauri Chaura, a peaceful demonstration in support of Gandhi's Home Rule campaign turns into an attack on the local police station. The mob sets fire to the building and, when the policemen who have been sheltering inside are forced to emerge, all are brutally hacked to death.

and there was an end to any form of protest. This he achieved.

However, despite his success, the British thought it prudent to arrest him and, once again, put him in prison. The charges put forward resulted in what is known as the Great Trial. Presided over by Judge Broomfield, the verdict on an accusation of sedition resulted in His Honour committing Gandhiji to prison for six years. In spite of this, he concluded his judgement with the remarkable statement, 'If, however, His Majesty's Government should, at some later date, see fit to reduce the term, no one would be better pleased than I.'

Gandhi did not in fact serve the full six years since he became ill and underwent an operation for appendicitis. He was released and allowed to recuperate in Juhu, just outside Bombay. Immediately Congress leaders flocked to see him, to discuss how the campaign should be reactivated. Gandhi's reply was typical. He had been convicted for six years and, had it not been for his illness and the compassion of the British authorities, he would still have been in prison. He would therefore take no part whatsoever in any action which could prove detrimental to the British until the entire six-year period had come to an end. When it did, however, there took place probably the most famous of all his massive campaigns of protest. Seventy-eight ashramites left the Sabarmati *ashram* outside Ahmedabad and marched some 240 miles to the beach at Dandi. There, the Mahatma*, as he was now known, ritually broke the law by picking up a handful of salt crystallised by the evaporation of sea water. It was illegal to manufacture or sell salt, except under licence from the British. By this symbolic march and simple act, Gandhiji exhorted all fellow Indians to follow his example and break the law. The result was extraordinary. The British authorities were totally incapable of coping with the scale of the protest. The whole salt campaign, culminating in the huge protest at the Dharasana Salt Works, resulted in the Viceroy, Lord Irwin, summoning Gandhiji to Viceregal Lodge to be informed of the setting up of the 1931 Conference to which he, Gandhi, was to be invited as the representative of the Indian Congress Party.

The Conference was in fact a sham. Britain's Prime Minister, Ramsay MacDonald, indulged in the policy of 'divide and rule', which had always been so successful in India. Gandhi was disillusioned but not surprised that Britain used the latent antagonism

* Mahatma: 'Great Soul'.

between Hindu and Muslim, and also between princely states, to erode the whole protest movement. Gandhiji believed passionately in Hindu/Muslim unity and campaigned for it endlessly but, in the years that followed, it became more and more evident that there were those within the country led, as ultimately became apparent, by Mohamed Ali Jinnah, who were determined to establish a separate Muslim state. This resulted in a partial fracturing of the Congress Party, although there remained within it a number of distinguished Muslims led, perhaps most prominently, and certainly with immense distinction, by the great Maulana Azad.

There also occurred now the manifestation of a further faction within the protest movement. This was led by Subhas Chandra Bose, who was convinced that Gandhi's non-violent concept was not only proving too slow, but indeed was likely to end in failure. So a whole new movement was established, resulting in the formation of the Indian National Army. In addition, Gandhiji had to cope with groups of young men, personified perhaps most dramatically by Bhagat Singh, who also believed that a form of violence employing those described as terrorists by one side, but as freedom fighters by the other, was the only way of achieving their ends.

When, in 1942, a British government mission, led by Sir Stafford Cripps, failed to satisfy the Congress leaders, Gandhi said, 'We can no longer hold back our people from exercising their will, nor can we go on eternally submitting to the imperialist policy. The time has come for the British to go.' The 'Quit India' resolution was proposed by Nehru, seconded by Patel, and passed by the Congress session in Bombay presided over by Azad.

Gandhi accompanied on a long walk along Juhu beach by Sushila Nayar, his personal physician. An archive photograph.

The British did not wait for a mass movement to gain ground. They arrested Gandhi, together with all the Congress leaders, and imprisoned him in the Aga Khan Palace at Pune with Kasturba, Mirabehn, Mahadev Desai and Sarojini Naidu. In February 1944, at the age of seventy-five, Kasturba died in Bapu's arms. Her death had been preceded, two years earlier, by that of his friend and principal secretary, Desai.

The war came to an end. The Congress leaders were released, Lord Wavell was relieved as Viceroy by Lord Louis Mountbatten, and the bitter negotiations for the cruel division of the country into Hindu India and Muslim Pakistan, known as Partition, began. Lord Louis had been granted total autonomy, and the right to set a date on which independence would be granted. It was set for August 1947 and the violence which was already in evidence between Hindu and Muslim erupted into a holocaust as Partition took its dreadful toll. Gandhiji's phenomenal courage in attempting to end the inter-religious bloodbath, particularly his crusade in Noakali, walking alone from village to village and stopping the strife, became the wonder of the world, and Lord

*Gandhi, devastated by the riot
at Chauri Chaura, announces
his intention of calling a halt
to the campaign for Home Rule
and of undertaking a fast to
end the wave of violence that
is erupting in India. The other
leaders (left to right) Patel,
Jinnah, Nehru and Azad
(Virendra Razdan) do their
best to dissuade him from such
a course, but Gandhi is adamant.*

*Kasturba knows that Gandhi is
close to death, due to the fast he
has undertaken as a penance.*

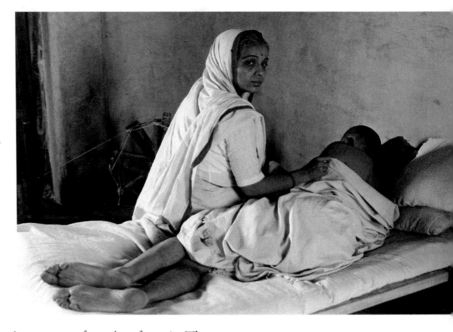

Louis referred to him as his 'one man frontier force'. The friendship, trust and love that Mountbatten and his wife Edwina had for Gandhiji was boundless and, indeed, Lord Louis was quoted as saying that 'In years to come, Mahatma Gandhi will go down in history on a par with Buddha and Jesus Christ.'

Two great fasts in Calcutta and Delhi as his last pleas to the populace to bury their hatred and live as brothers resulted in Gandhiji's near death. Ultimately they brought the violence virtually to an end. Gandhi had crusaded constantly for the treatment of Hindu and Muslim on equal terms, culminating in his persuading the Government of India to make massive financial contributions to aid those Muslims who had fled from India and were now attempting to re-establish their lives in the new state of Pakistan. This was the last straw for the Hindu extremists.

On 30 January 1948, in Delhi, Gandhiji was assassinated by a young man called Godse, a Hindu who believed that the Mahatma was defiling the highest ethics of the Hindu religion.

On hearing of his assassination, the grief the world experienced was almost unique. The tributes paid were without reservation.

99

As a gesture of ultimate respect, the United Nations halted its deliberations as soon as the news reached New York. As Einstein had said, 'It may be that in years to come men will scarce believe that one such as this ever in flesh and blood walked upon this earth.' Gandhiji was cremated at Rajghat, on the outskirts of Delhi, and his ashes scattered at the confluence of the Ganges and the Jumna at Allahabad.

This brief and simplified version of Gandhiji's life comprises elements which do not appear in the final film. In addition, there are whole aspects of the story which, after much discussion, Gerry and I had already decided to omit for reasons of length. There was the question of Gandhiji's relationship with his four

An archive photograph of Gandhi with Lord and Lady Louis Mountbatten during discussions at the Viceregal palace about India's future in 1947.

children, culminating in the tragedy of Harilal, the oldest son, denouncing his father, becoming Muslim, and arriving at his mother's deathbed drunk. There was also the question, which so many detractors and commentators have blown up out of all proportion, regarding Gandhi's testing of the vow of *brahmacharya* in the latter years of his life. I personally believe, as a result of my many discussions with those who knew him, that he never broke his solemn undertaking in this respect.

Neither have I gone into the levels of debate in relation to Gandhi's 'experiments with truth': his search for the truth, his attempt to understand the meaning of the Infinite, as he put it, to see God face to face—his conviction that truth was God and therefore God was truth—his broad social concerns and his advocacy of a constructive programme for the encouragement of village industry; his fight for the rights of women; his determination to eradicate untouchability, and above all his ultimate goal to alleviate the cruel poverty which spanned the Indian sub-continent. Poverty, he said, is the worst form of violence.

Gerry and I discussed and deliberated hour after hour, day after day. We eventually arrived at the conclusion that the form and line our film should take should be to follow Gandhiji's own life, and concentrate upon those events, circumstances and relationships which touched directly upon his existence, setting aside all others, no matter how momentous, which did not directly affect him. We were not telling the story of the formation and intricacies of the Congress Party. We were not even telling the story of the struggle for Independence. We were not debating Gandhiji's views in regard to the conflict between industrialisation and village industries. We were attempting to discover, and then dramatise, the spirit of this extraordinary man.

In its original form, Gerry's script contained the outline set out in the previous paragraphs. It also incorporated much detail of Gandhi's first trip to London in the 1880s, and followed to some extent the lives of his children. But these sequences were discarded at a very early stage purely on grounds of length. Of one thing we were certain: the film should start with the assassination. It seemed essential that, for vast numbers of people throughout the world, a knowledge of who and what Gandhiji became was a prerequisite to understanding and wishing to follow the story of his life. Only in retrospect, in the knowledge of the extraordinary awe in which he was finally held by the world at large, would the pertinence of his struggles and heart-searching achieve its full effect.

Gerry during this period wrote like a man possessed. Surrounded by all his research material, piles of books, heaps of notes, pouring coffee endlessly down his throat, he would work with a concentration which I found remarkable. He would periodically take off, disappear, perhaps to be found late at night at the India Club but, more often than not, absent for some three or four days on a blinder, returning, Heaven knows how, refreshed and ready to start again on his mammoth task. He eventually, in December, delivered the script, which incorporated one or two minor revisions we'd agreed upon at the last moment. It seemed inordinately long, even to me, and so I had it timed at once. I wrote to Gerry to tell him of the result, and received a letter written on New Year's Eve, 1963, which began, 'My dear dear Dickie, Five hours!!! Santa Madonna. Is it possible? It can't be. What can we take out? 60 pages at least! Dio Mio etc!'

He was right, and we faced but one of the gigantic problems that beset us in making *Gandhi*: that of achieving a successful condensation of the story to within something like three hours.

During the latter part of 1963, I had meetings with three

In the Circuit Court at Ahmedabad, Judge Broomfield presides over Gandhi's trial and, from the very outset, displays strong personal views on the prisoner before him and the crime of sedition with which he is charged. Contrary to all legal precedent, it is Judge Broomfield who rises respectfully to his feet as Gandhi – the prisoner – enters the dock.

Directing Trevor Howard, who plays Judge Broomfield

people, all of whom, in their own way, had a significant influence on the progress of the project.

The first was Horace Alexander, the English Quaker who had been such an advocate of Gandhiji both in his public utterances and in his many writings. He knew Gandhi well during the last twenty years of his life and visited him in India on a number of occasions. Mr Alexander was a great supporter of the project, and gave me, at a time when it was greatly needed, the degree of assurance that I required about the propriety of making a film about such a figure.

The second person was to play a very considerable part in seeing the film ultimately launched. I was approached, once knowledge of the project was made public, to do a radio interview for the BBC Hindi Service. I happily agreed, and met for the first time Rani Dube. She eventually became the co-producer of the film, and in no small measure she was responsible for the final mounting of the production in India, both in terms of her entrée to government departments, and the advocacy which she brought to bear in persuading various government officials to back the project, with their considerable influence and authority. She was an extremely attractive, bright young woman and greatly knowledgeable about Gandhiji's life, caring deeply for all his beliefs.

I also met Muriel Lester, the engaging woman who created and ran Kingsley Hall in the East End of London, the community centre at which Gandhiji stayed during his time in London for the 1931 Conference. She had touching and revealing stories to tell of the informal and unrecorded part of Gandhiji's lifestyle. I determined then that if it was viable at all I would include in the film a scene, however brief, commemorating that particular sojourn, and I am delighted that it proved to be possible.

As had been agreed, I sent the first part of the revised script to Alec Guinness and I received, sadly, a letter which made it perfectly clear that he felt, after most deep and considered thought, that playing Gandhi was not something that he could undertake. He wrote of the script, 'I think it is both tender and interesting, and has the authentic ring of truth about it, and I do congratulate you and Gerald Hanley greatly. But, my dear Dickie, I honestly believe that you can do much better than me. I still think you need an Indian, but there may well be an English name—Finney, perhaps, or even no name at all. I know how this will disappoint you. You have been so sweetly encouraging and enthusiastic, but I feel it dishonest to let it slide further into possibility, because I am too old, too grey-eyed, too heavy and just plain too old. My love to you always, Alec.'

It was such a typically straightforward and truthful letter, the sort of letter that one would anticipate receiving from Alec. But it was, nevertheless, a bitter blow—one I had to accept, and one I would have to reveal, particularly to Pandit Nehru, who had been so enthusiastic about the idea of Alec playing Gandhiji.

My second trip to India, this time, happily, with Moti and Sheila, was now imminent. I wrote and sent telegrams to Mr Khanna, telling him of our arrival, and asking again to meet the Prime Minister and Mrs Gandhi. As previously, we received a charming reply, saying that the Prime Minister would be happy to see us at 12.30 on Wednesday, 20 November in Parliament House. It was our intention not only to see the Prime Minister, but also to meet a number of the new ministers who had in the interim been appointed. We planned to spend a week or so in various parts of India as well, particularly looking at the Sabarmati *ashram* on the outskirts of Ahmedabad, to examine the possibilities of shooting in those areas, returning finally to Delhi in the hope that in the meantime the Prime Minister might have had a chance to look through the script.

We left London Airport on Tuesday, 19 November. On our

arrival, Moti and I paid our long-anticipated ceremonial visit together to Rajghat and then checked into our hotel. In the afternoon I went to see Rajkumari Amrit Kaur—on the last occasion when I was in Delhi, she had been abroad. Lord Louis was very anxious that I should meet her, since he felt that her knowledge of Gandhiji in the period during which she was his principal private secretary might be very valuable to me. His instinct was correct. There were, even then, few people alive who had known Gandhiji intimately. Talks with Pandit Nehru had of course been phenomenally valuable and my relatively brief time with Horace Alexander had helped to paint in further little details of Bapu's character. But here was someone who had worked with Gandhiji for over a decade. She was an aristocrat, a princess in fact, tall, almost regal in bearing, very beautiful and dressed exquisitely. She was eager to know all I could tell her about the film. Like so many others, she obviously had a tremendous love for Bapu and because of that was deeply anxious that we should do justice to a man whom she felt was as great as any human being that had lived on this earth. She talked to me about his enduring gentleness, his wonderful sense of humour, his meticulousness, his belief in the vital conservation of all things, down to the smallest scrap of paper—letters written on the inside of used envelopes—to the last little stub of pencil. Overriding everything, though, she conveyed his deep love for his fellow human beings. She wanted me to meet other Indian leaders who had known him well—Rajagopalachari, Jayaprakash Narayan, Acharya Kripalani and Abdul Ghaffar Khan—and was really quite distressed that I had not already made plans to see them. In fact, I did finally have the opportunity of meeting the last two. At the end of our talk, the proud possessor of an enchanting little book she had written about Bapu and which she signed for me, I returned to the hotel and bed.

With Ben Kingsley, a study in concentration.

The following day, Moti and I presented ourselves at Parliament House. I was really quite shocked to see the Prime Minister. It was only some six months since I had last met him, but he seemed to have aged markedly. He did not seem at all well, but, nevertheless, despite whatever effort was required, he summoned up his usual warmth in greeting us and enquiring as to the progress of our project. He was obviously enormously busy and we only stayed for a short time, leaving with him a copy of the script in the hope that he might perhaps be able to look at it before our next meeting.

He had already made it possible for us to meet a number of the members of his Cabinet. We saw the Minister of Finance, Mr Krishnamachari, who was most helpful, and immediately made arrangements for us to pay our expenses and air fares (provided we flew Air India) with rupee finance. His joint secretary, Mr Y. T. Shah, facilitated the opening of an Indo-British bank account in India, which required Ministry of Finance approval. We also met Manobhai Shah, the Minister of International Trade, who offered us every co-operation he could, and finally Mr Narain Sinha, the new Minister of Information and Broadcasting who, although not at all well, called to see us at a little party Jackie Baroda gave us before we left Delhi for our reconnaissance trip.

Jackie described his discussions with Mr Y. B. Chavan, the Minister of Defence, who also said that he would see that any requirements we had related to the Forces would be dealt with expeditiously.

Jack Rix was a very experienced Production Controller and we had worked together on a number of occasions, particularly on *The Angry Silence*. I had asked him if he would be good enough to come to India to advise me on what he felt the primary obstacles might be in attempting this production—in fact, to tell me whether, in his opinion, it was really viable. Needless to say I had no money to pay him a salary, but that made no difference to Jack. On mere provision of air fares for himself and his wife, Joy, he came out and did a most valuable recce assessment, preceding us to the Sabarmati *ashram*, outside Ahmedabad, set on the bank quite high above the river.

Our visit there was another of those occasions which I shall never forget. Despite the formalisation of the site, with its railings and notices and concrete-paved paths and signs as to where one might go and not go, it was still extraordinarily evocative of all that I had imagined Gandhi's *ashram* to be. Naturally it had been described to me by a number of people, and I had read everything I could lay my hands on, but now there it was suddenly in front of me. I think my overwhelming impression was one of peace. There was nothing in its construction, in its setting, in its colour, that jarred: the colours were pastel as if literally crayonned with the delicacy of a Monet. Of one thing I was certain. This must be the model that we used as the principal *ashram* in our film. Factually, there were several in Gandhi's life in India; Sabarmati, Sevagram and ultimately Wardha, but obviously in such a short space of screen time it would be impossible to establish all of them satis-

Rehearsing the lakeside scene in which Rohini Hattangady, who plays Kasturba, and Ben Kingsley, who plays Mahatma, re-enact their marriage.

factorily. So we would have to decide on one *ashram*, even despite Gandhiji's statement that if the Dandi salt march failed to achieve its objective, he would never return to Sabarmati until Independence had been attained.

By great good fortune, we had the opportunity of meeting Chaganlal Gandhi, Bapu's second cousin, who lived there. He must have been well into his eighties and, although very bent and almost toothless, still conveyed a zest for life and pleasure at meeting someone who was interested in his famous relative.

I wanted to start pacing out the dimensions of the site, to have an art director with me, to start talking of how we might construct it, but of course this was all very premature and I had to content myself with merely taking pictures and discussing with Jack our ability to recreate it as a film set. This would obviously be a major part of our building costs, as there was no possibility, even if one had been given permission, of using the actual Sabarmati site. The conversion that had taken place, turning it into a form of museum, would rule out any possibility of making it resemble the original *ashram*, constructed over forty years beforehand.

We returned to Delhi. Before leaving for the *ashram*, we had also arranged for a script to be delivered to Mrs Gandhi and both Moti and I went to see her to learn of her reactions. They were, I suppose, what one would anticipate. She thought it very good, as far as it went. She was concerned about one or two major elements which were not included. She felt that certain emphases were perhaps not as she would have chosen and she told us there were a number of inaccuracies. In general, however, she was approving and thought that the overall construction was eminently successful.

We then had a meeting with Panditji. On this occasion, we met him at Teen Murti, in the same room where Vala and I had first met Indiraji. We were very much aware of the pressures on the Prime Minister, almost overwhelming at this particular time, and I was most anxious that the meeting should not take any longer than was absolutely necessary. I thanked him first for arranging the various appointments with his Cabinet Ministers and told him of their offers of co-operation and assistance. Most particularly, I mentioned Mr Narain Sinha's statement that, provided there was no objection to the final screenplay, then the Ministry of Information and Broadcasting, to whom we would be primarily responsible, would grant us every possible help.

The Prime Minister said that he had had the opportunity of looking at the script but, owing to pressure of work, had not read it very thoroughly. However, he felt that we should give a great deal of thought to the selection of the principal figures we ultimately decided to portray in the film. He readily accepted that it would be impossible to include all the main statesmen involved in the Indian struggle for Independence, or even all the main British figures who participated. He was totally opposed to merely dragging in a series of names by somewhat cursory reference, just to have them mentioned. He felt that we should settle on a relatively small number of people and allow them, in a way, to represent all the major figures concerned. He certainly thought that Sardar Patel was essential, and also Maulana Azad. It went, of course, without saying that Mohamed Ali Jinnah would have to be involved. He particularly liked the early sequences, and the period in South Africa. He felt it illustrated most graphically the gradual development of Gandhiji's character and philosophies, which determined ultimately all his major actions in India. He accepted the necessity in a film to concertina—to truncate events —to construct circumstances in which certain debates and ultimate resolutions could be staged dramatically and succinctly; events, in fact, which probably occurred over a period of time and, even then, possibly merely by correspondence. He was not at all convinced that slavishly following the minute details of chronology would necessarily result in the overall effect that we were attempting to achieve. He was certain that most important of all was to discover a way of conveying Gandhi's spirit—if we

*American newsman, Walker,
played by Martin Sheen.*

were able to do that, he said, then the whole concept of the film would be justified. He told us that he intended to send this first draft to D. G. Tendulkar, the author of the eight-volume *Mahatma*, but that he was not at all sure as to this particular decision at the moment. He knew that we had already met B. R. Nanda, the author of the most recent biography on Gandhi, and we told him that we had spent several hours with Mr Nanda, going over a number of reservations and criticisms that he had on the script, most of which we were anxious to incorporate.

He then asked us if there was any news of Alec Guinness, and I had to confess that, certainly for the present, Alec had said no. He thought this was a great pity, since he believed that Alec had the right personality to play Bapu. I asked him whether, in principle, he felt that it was acceptable, and would be acceptable to India as a whole, that their great leader might be played by an Englishman. He hesitated for a moment, and then replied, with an impish grin, that should it finally prove to be the case, it would make Gandhiji laugh a great deal.

But on discussing the conundrum more seriously, he said he felt that the development of skills and the technique of Indian artists — and one must remember this was 1963 — were not of a sufficient calibre to be likely to throw up a figure capable of undertaking this mammoth task, covering, as it did, for the actor, at least sixty years. He thought under such circumstances the experience of a classical English actor, trained in the theatre and accepting a totally naturalistic style of performance, would be invaluable. Indeed, he questioned whether the film would be possible if we were not able ultimately to engage an English actor of the requisite stature to play the part. However, the final decision, he said, in all these matters must be one for those who were making the film. He was anxious that we should listen to the views and advice which, laughingly, he said he knew would be plentiful, but we must be sure in our own minds that what arrived on the screen, in the final analysis, was what we wished to say.

It seemed to me that these views, expressed by someone who was so very intimately involved in the events that we were hoping to portray, were quite exceptional. I suppose, really, it was no more than one would anticipate from such a man. There is no doubt in my mind that of the number of great figures that I have had the privilege of knowing over the years, none impressed me more deeply than Pandit Nehru.

We took our leave and he came to the door to say goodbye. I

was just about to get into the taxi when he made one further observation. 'Whatever you do,' he said, 'do not deify him—that is what we have done in India—and he was too great a *man* to be deified.'

If there is one observation, one statement, that has been my touchstone throughout the attempt to make *Gandhi*, it is this. Those words were to be the last that Pandit Nehru ever spoke to me, and I shall always be grateful to him, not only for them, but for his unique contribution in making the film possible.

Moti and I still had a number of matters to deal with before we left India. What we did not anticipate was the statement a few days later made by the Prime Minister in the Rajha Sabha.

He said, 'I have had a number of talks with Mr Richard Attenborough and, in my judgement, the British producer is mentally equipped to undertake the production and strikes me as a good man for this work.'

We left for London, as might be imagined, in high spirits.

Gandhi revisits Porbandar, his birth place and plans a new act of defiance against the British. He promises Walker, the American journalist who has travelled many thousands of miles in search of a story, that he will not be disappointed.

5   The year did not end, however, on quite such a joyous note. During our time in Delhi, we had seen quite a lot of Jackie Baroda and his associate, Bobby Kadam. Everything appeared to be going ahead without reservation, and Jackie was still extremely enthusiastic about the project.

However, in the last week of December Moti and I received a copy of a letter that he had written to Bobby Kadam which said that certain unforeseen financial liabilities had been forced upon him, which made it well nigh impossible for him to think of going through with the project. It was a severe blow. Without the Indian financing our ability to raise further funds in order to proceed with the second draft of the script was considerably impaired. Moti and I therefore agreed that we should do everything in our power to persuade Jackie, even if only for the present, to withdraw his letter. This he subsequently did, but only for a limited period. I had had a meeting with Earl St John and Mike Stanley-Evans at Pinewood on the day prior to receiving this news. They were delighted with the progress that had been made in India, and agreed to discuss with John Davis the possibility of further funds, even if they were somewhat limited, to help finance a second draft.

In the middle of January I received a disappointing letter from the Secretary to the Minister of Information and Broadcasting, Mr Nawab Singh. Having had such a warm reception from the Prime Minister, followed by his announcement in the Rajha Sabha, I had anticipated this letter being unreserved in its offers of assistance and co-operation. It read: 'I write to inform you that we have *no objection* to your going ahead with your preparations for the film on the life of the Mahatma Gandhi, subject to the final script being found satisfactory by the Government of India. If the script on submission is found unexceptionable, there will be no difficulty about *usual assistance being supplied.*' (The italics are mine.) Obviously, this was very much less than I had hoped for and placed the assurances that I had given Earl St John and Mike Stanley-Evans in some doubt. I decided that once more I had to seek the help of Lord Louis. As before, the timing could not have been more fortunate, since he was again about to leave for New Delhi. I explained exactly what had happened, and he immediately saw the problem, undertaking to discuss the situation with Pandit Nehru.

Subsequently I received a phone call from Earl St John to say that he had talked to John Davis, who was not averse to giving further assistance, but felt very strongly that a contribution in some form should be made on our part. I went to see Richard Gregson, Gerry Hanley's agent, and it was agreed that Gerry would agree to write the second draft, which would take him approximately four months, but that he would defer a considerable proportion of his salary, which would be paid only if the film finally went ahead. Together with that, I would also put in a further sum of money so that Gerry and I, between us, would be supplying, in one form or another, the greater proportion of the total sum required to proceed.

Fortunately, from my point of view, just after Christmas I had been sent a Robert Hollis screenplay by a friend of many years' standing, the film producer George Brown. It was called *Guns at Batasi*. He was offering me the part of a regimental sergeant

I demonstrate a respectful pranam *for villagers to emulate as Ben Kingsley strides past during the filming of the Salt March.*

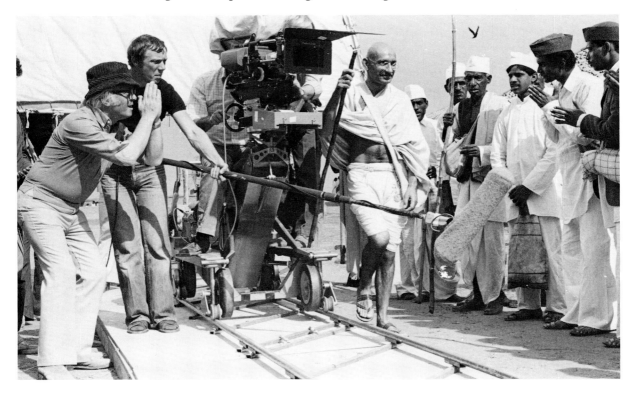

Gandhi is about to embark on the historic Salt March of 1930. As newsreel cameras and journalists from all over the world prepare to record the occasion, the Mahatma's followers stand ready to follow him some 240 miles to the beach at Dandi. There, on the anniversary of the Jallianwala Bagh massacre, Gandhi will ritually break the law by gathering untaxed salt from the seashore.

major. It was, I think, probably as effective a role as I had been offered since Pinkie in *Brighton Rock*, and I was very anxious indeed to play it. As circumstances turned out, it was of course more than just a good part. It meant that, with the salary that I would receive, I could afford to invest further money in the Gandhi film.

A letter arrived from the Minister of Information and Broadcasting, enclosing various notes from Mr Tendulkar about the screenplay. There were, inevitably, a number of mere factual corrections, which he said should be rectified. He also felt that the balance between Southern Africa and India from 1915 onwards was incorrect. He believed that the London and Southern African sections should be greatly reduced, since the complexities and significance of Gandhiji's achievements in India far outweighed the earlier ones. I personally felt that this was an over-simplification of the situation. It seemed to me that, without understanding the processes and experiences Gandhiji under-went in order to form his character and attitudes, the actual achievements in India lost a great deal of their poignancy. Gerry was due back in London any day, staying again at the India Club, and Moti and I would be discussing these various views with him.

In the first week of February, I received a wonderfully reassur-ing letter from Lord Louis, written from Rangoon, and sent to us via the diplomatic bag. He had had a most successful meeting with Pandit Nehru and his daughter. He had explained the difficulties that we were facing with the officials in the various ministries who, not unnaturally, were reluctant to give any more assurances and undertakings in their communications than were, in their opinion, absolutely necessary. It appeared that Mr Nehru had one or two quite pertinent things to say, not only about certain ministries, but also in regard to the views and criticisms made by the various people who had by now read the script. He had also said that I must, without question, be my own judge as to what would make the best film.

Lord Louis had explained my reluctance to approach the Prime Minister himself whenever I appeared to be facing some obstacle, and they decided that a person of some standing should be nominated by Panditji to represent him in this particular matter. The suggestion was that the representative should be Indira, and apparently she immediately expressed her willingness to take on this responsibility. Not only at that particular time, but indeed as future events turned out, this decision could, from our point of view, scarcely have been more propitious. Lord Louis had, once again, come to our rescue.

I was by now in full preparation for *Batasi*. To play RSM Lauderdale I really had to look like an efficient member of Her Majesty's Forces. I therefore enlisted the invaluable help of the

At the age of 61, setting a break-neck pace, Gandhi is joined by thousands of followers on his way to the sea at Dandi during the famous Salt March.

As Regimental Sergeant Major Lauderdale in Guns at Batasi.

celebrated RSM Britten. I trained with the Coldstream Guards at Chelsea Barracks and spent hour after hour, not only drilling under the RSM's withering gaze, but also retraining my voice in order to bark my commands across any parade ground in the land. Shooting began at the end of February and continued until the beginning of May.

Gerry and I started our regular meetings again and when I came home each evening I would spend as much time as possible going over the new construction with him and examining in some detail the re-adjudged scenes as he wrote them.

It was marvellous to be acting again. RSM Lauderdale was a terrific part, and I felt ready to play him. The preparation I had done was very thorough and Berman's had, as usual, provided me with a superb costume. I felt comfortable and confident. The director, John Guillerman, gave me a tremendous amount of help and encouragement. Jack Hawkins made a guest appearance and the other star of the film was Flora Robson. It was the first time I had acted with Dame Flora. I cannot say how impressed I was by the quality and truth of everything she did. Britt Ekland was to have played the young female lead but, because of various stormy romantic complications with Peter Sellers, her husband of only a few weeks, she suddenly left the production. The result was that a few mornings later a little enchantress by the name of Mia Farrow appeared on the set to play opposite Johnny Leyton. It was her first film. She won everybody's heart including, in the quite near future, that of Frank Sinatra. Sheila and I happened to be in Hollywood at that time, and were amongst the guests at their wedding party given by Bill and Edie Goetz.

Persuaded by Pandit Nehru's views, I wrote yet once again to Alec Guinness, who had just opened to a huge success in *Dylan* at the Plymouth Theatre in New York, to ask if he had by any chance had a change of heart in regard to playing Gandhi. His reply was charming but negative, and Moti and I had no option but to accept this situation as final.

It was early in 1964 that I learnt of the death of Rajkumari Amrit Kaur. This was a great sadness, not only because I had been looking forward to seeing her again enormously, but because she had promised me a considerable amount of her time filling in details of the daily life and routine of Gandhi during his last ten years or so.

I was still very preoccupied with the situation as far as Jackie Baroda was concerned. If he pulled out, then our position with the Rank Organisation was quite untenable. Moti's determination was unshakeable, and it was decided that he would go to Delhi to see Jackie. Although Moti never made a great song and dance about it, I think he had a fairly tough time. As I have learnt, Jackie tends to postpone meetings and change arrangements frequently, and I am certain that Moti found the negotiations very frustrating. However, at the beginning of March I had received a telegram from him, saying that a new agreement had been concluded with Jackie in which he reiterated his genuine interest in the project and to this end would provide the necessary rupee finance. Moti returned in triumph.

On 25 April the second script, still, I fear, considerably over-length, was completed, and sent off to John Davis. Now everything depended on the reaction of the Rank Organisation. If this was favourable, it did seem there was every chance we could go ahead. But then, on 27 May, the tragedy which one felt had been imminent for some months occurred. Pandit Nehru died.

There is little doubt that the problems, both national and international, particularly those in Goa and the hostilities with China, contributed to the deterioration of his health. He was a tremendous loss, not only to India, but to the human race. He was a most civilised man and, as Gerry Hanley said in a note to me, 'a world person'. I wrote immediately of course to Indiraji, Mrs Pandit, Lord Louis and to Panditji's secretaries, Mr Khanna and Mr Ram. Everyone acknowledged the letters, but I received from Mr Ram and Mr Khanna two very touching, quite long, hand-written replies. Their sense of loss, expressed in such unreserved terms, for a man they had — and I use their word — served for so many years, was as fine a tribute to the late Prime Minister as any for which he might have hoped.

As far as the film was concerned, this of course was a considerable blow. Whilst in no way belittling his daughter's contribution and advocacy, the fact remained that it was Pandit Nehru who first publicly approved of the project and I felt it insensitive to press Indiraji at this particular time.

A further setback was to follow. After a number of postponements, I finally saw John Davis again. He told me that, although he admired the script greatly and thought the subject to be of some importance, his original reservations were in fact confirmed. He doubted the commercial viability of the project; he feared greatly for our ability to make the film in India; and in any event, he was certain that the budget would ultimately prove to be prohibitive as far as the Rank Organisation was concerned.

Lal Bahandra Shastri had been elected the second Prime Minister of India. We learnt early in June that he had invited Mrs Gandhi to become the Minister of Information and Broadcasting, and that she had accepted this Cabinet position. From our point of view, of course, this was most fortunate, in that, having been the only other person present at a number of our vital discussions with Mr Nehru, she was now the Minister primarily responsible for film production.

About a month after Pandit Nehru died I met Louis Fischer. He was a big man, and the smooth wisp of hair that had covered a small part of his otherwise bald pate in the only photograph I had seen of him was now non-existent—but he still had an outer rim of white hair, rather like Gandhiji himself when he was in his seventies. He spoke with a soft American accent and gave the impression that life was so well worth living, one should enjoy and experience every moment of it to the full. Moti, of course, had known him for some time. Fischer had been so excited at the prospect of a film being made on the life of Gandhi that, in order to encourage and help Moti, he had agreed to allow him to purchase the film rights in his two books for the princely sum of £1. He had arrived in London unexpectedly, and was staying for only a day or so. I longed to have a relaxed period of time with him, but it was not possible. However, even during the few hours that we were together, he answered my myriad questions with a flow of detailed information that was almost too much to assimilate. I was left with the impression, though, that, of all the world leaders he had met over the years, there was no doubt whatsoever Mahatma Gandhi was the most impressive figure he had ever come across.

Once more, through Moti's entreaties, Jackie Baroda had extended his period of commitment to the rupee expenditure of the production, on this occasion to December 31. Despite the tragedy of Pandit Nehru's death, all other circumstances seemed propitious, if only we were able to find the non-rupee finance.

It was then, on 7 July, that I met the person who, for fifteen years or so, was to dominate all the multifarious schemes and proposals that seemed at the time likely to see the film go into production. His name was Joseph E. Levine.

I had been bemoaning my frustrations to my agent, Johnny Redway, and he introduced me to an American producer named Ronnie Kahn. Ronnie said, 'I know exactly the person you

should meet. He is an absolute genius at mounting unusual movies. He's coming to London and I will arrange for you to see him.' My appointment was at 10.30 on Tuesday, 7 July, at Claridges. I had no idea what he'd look like — indeed, I wasn't really sure quite what to expect when I arrived. The scene, however, was such that if I had asked for the archetypal Hollywood to be translated to this most dignified of London hotels, the result, I'm sure, would not have disappointed me. The suite was huge, and it seemed in each corner of the sitting-room there were separate

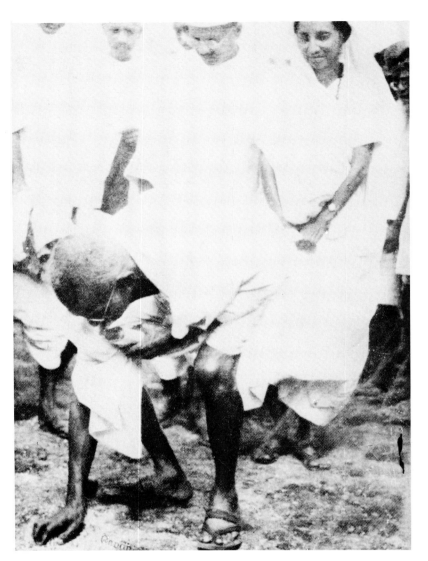

Gandhi gathers up salt from the beach at Dandi during his 1930 campaign to break the government monopoly. An archive photograph.

groups of people accompanied by their lawyers and advisers, all working on possible deals. As if that was not enough, I gradually became aware of the fact that there were two further coveys wheeling and dealing in the adjoining bedroom. Between long-distance phone calls, like some cruising dreadnought, Joe Levine glided from group to group, dropping personal observations into their deliberations as he sailed past. Almost without stopping, his first words to me were, 'Why the hell do you want to make a film about Gandhi?' (I seemed to have heard those words somewhere before!) The fact that he had scarcely paused, fortunately, gave me a moment to try and compose an answer. It must, I feel, have been reasonably satisfactory since, by the end of the morning, matters had progressed to the point where Joe Levine had agreed to finance a major research trip to India, and also to assume the financial obligations that Moti and I had already undertaken.

We had a series of meetings with Joe during the three days that he was in town, enormously assisted by his London representative, Kenneth Hargreaves. I, of course, over the succeeding years, came to know Joe very well—as well as it is possible for anybody to know him. He's a buccaneer. All the giant moguls in the film industry have gone, but Joe remains, obdurate and imperishable, a man of massive courage, with an ability to promote and sell both his product and himself that can surely never have been equalled. Fearlessly independent, ruthless in obtaining what he believes is necessary for a particular project, tireless, inventive, with a wonderfully ingenuous excitement about the cinema, he is truly the stuff of which magic is made. If he is fond of someone, there is almost nothing he will not do for them. On the other hand, one has to say, if you fall out of favour or, worse still, if you cross him, God help you!

He left for Los Angeles with the script in his bag and all the various legal and financial information that was required to set the negotiations in progress. He was to discuss the matter with Paramount, with whom he now had a mammoth production deal and, provided they agreed with his views—and it would take a brave man to oppose them—an announcement would be made that Joseph E. Levine would be presenting a film called *Mahatma Gandhi*, directed, as his first assignment, by the English actor/producer, Richard Attenborough.

Indira Gandhi came to London towards the end of July 1964 as part of the Indian delegation attending the Commonwealth Prime Ministers' conference. Moti and I went to see her, on the 20th of that month, at Claridges. She was naturally very thrilled at the sudden surge forward that had been made in our production plans, with the intended participation of Joe Levine's company, Embassy Pictures, and Paramount. We told her that we were soon to meet with our various lawyers in New York, together with the Maharaja of Baroda and his advisers, and that if everything developed satisfactorily, a press release would be issued announcing that the film would start actual production, hopefully on the 96th anniversary of Mahatma Gandhi's birth, 2 October 1965. Moti and his lawyer, Laurence Harbottle, who was also acting for Indo-British Films in these negotiations, left for New York a couple of days before I did, in order that they might have

Gandhi's arrest does not stop a planned protest demonstration at the British-controlled salt works in Dharasana, led now by Azad and Sarojini Naidu (Tarla Mehta).

OPPOSITE

At Dharasana a huge orderly column of Gandhians clad in white homespun prepares to march forward, six at a time, and confront a strong police guard at the salt works gate, each wielding the potentially lethal weighted bamboo stave known as a lathi.

some preparatory meetings with Jackie Baroda and Boddy Kadam. Johnny Redway and I followed on the 24th.

Joe had already told us that Paramount had warmly welcomed the concept of the film. As a result, we anticipated that our discussions in New York would be not only constructive, but immensely positive. This proved to be the case.

One question that did arise during our talks was my availability to push forward with the very considerable programme of pre-production activity in order to meet our first day of shooting. I had been asked to play in an MGM picture called *Operation Crossbow*, and I had promised on my return to discover whether I could obtain a reasonable stop date. It became apparent very quickly that this was not possible. Although I could well have done with the income, I took the decision to give up this picture in order to devote myself entirely to the Gandhi film. Moti was in a similar frame of mind, and decided that, with negotiations proceeding apace, he too ought to devote his full time to the production. He therefore decided to resign from his position at the High Commission on 1 November.

I wrote to John Davis to tell him that I imagined the negotiations with Embassy would be completed within the next few weeks, and that he could anticipate receiving the repayment of the £7,000 that he had advanced, together with the accrued interest.

It was now essential for Moti and me to return to India, not only to verify all the various approvals and permissions that had been granted, but also to obtain from the Ministry of Finance the assurances that Embassy and Paramount required as far as the Baroda investment was concerned.

Moti left a day or so before me, since I remained in London for

the première of *Batasi*. The following day I flew to Delhi. I had once again asked for Lord Louis' assistance in arranging various appointments. In particular I of course wished to pay my respects to the new Prime Minister, and Lord Louis also suggested that I should take the opportunity of meeting Dr Radakrishnan, the President of India. Mr Shastri, Pandit Nehru's successor, was really quite tiny, dressed in the traditional Congress Party white *khadi** with his little Gandhi cap. He struck me as being possibly as close to the true Gandhian figure as anyone I had so far met. He, too, gave our project his absolute approval, and reiterated the Government's pleasure at the thought of a 'serious film'—as it was referred to in India—being made on the life of the Mahatma. Dr Radakrishnan, although an obvious Gandhian devotee, was a very different figure: tall, extremely dignified, wearing a most beautiful turban. He received us in his private rooms in Rashtrapati Bhavan, the building that was formerly the Viceroy's residence. He gave us tea and we told him of our plans. Again, unqualified co-operation was offered. We explained to him that it might well be necessary to shoot a number of sequences both inside and outside the building. He foresaw no difficulty and indeed said that, as far as he was concerned, we might make total use of Rashtrapati Bhavan, provided only that such scenes had historically taken place in the building.

We saw Mrs Gandhi again and discussed the script with her once more. Moti also took me to meet a quite enchanting man, Mr R. R. Diwakar, who was the Chairman of the Gandhi Smarak Nidi, the principal Gandhian foundation. He too gave the film his blessing, but wished to see the screenplay before offering any practical assistance.

Our intention had been to conclude our arrangements in India within two or three weeks. In fact we stayed there, with just a brief three days back in London, for more than six weeks. I remember sending a telegram home saying, 'Making miserably slow progress, but not without hope.' We had intended to announce the film in Delhi, but because of delays in obtaining the official approval of the rupee investment and the difficulty of getting the relevant personalities to India, we decided on a change of plan for our announcement. The press reception was switched to the Savoy Hotel in London, and the date to 15 December.

We returned to a series of the discussions and correspondence

* *Khadi*: cotton homespun cloth

124

September 1964: in Delhi, Moti and I show Gerald Hanley's script to Indira Gandhi, three months after her appointment as Minister of Information and Broadcasting.

which seem inevitably to surround the contractual agreements required in the mounting of a film production. Each party employs its advisers, lawyers, accountants, tax consultants, and invariably what ought to be a relatively simple arrangement between two groups of people turns into a major drama. Certainly the Embassy lawyers required further assurances than they had requested at our initial meeting. It meant that even on the day of the press conference questions relating to governmental approvals, the release of rupees, the right of Jackie Baroda to invest in the film at all, the allocation of profits related to the investors as against the production company, and the whole principle of a salary for Moti were still up in the air.

We invited people who had been involved in our efforts so far: Mrs Gandhi, Louis Fischer, Jackie Baroda, Mr Diwakar and Lord Louis. None of them was able to attend, but Lord Louis was good enough to send me a telegram: 'I am very sorry that, owing to my absence with the Secretary of State for Defence at the NATO Council meeting in Paris, I am unable to be present at your press conference today. I am more than happy that this film is to be made as I have taken a keen personal interest in the preliminary arrangements. Indeed, I discussed the whole project with the late Prime Minister of India. I am quite sure we are going to see in due course a truly first-class film, and I should like to take this opportunity of wishing you the very best of good fortune in your project. Mountbatten of Burma.'

Described in the now defunct *Daily Cinema* as 'one of the largest and most enthusiastic press receptions seen in London for many years', the Savoy's River Restaurant seemed absolutely packed with people facing a large formal table and microphones set at one end. Fortunately, our guests did include Muriel Lester from Kingsley Hall and Mr and Mrs Horace Alexander: the Deputy High Commissioner was also present. But one of the hosts was not. Joe Levine, who certainly never misses a press conference if he can help it, was detained in Los Angeles. Lenny Lightstone, Vice-President of Embassy Pictures, and Ken Hargreaves, Embassy's executive in London, had to represent the company in his stead. Joe was the Producer, Moti the Executive Producer, and myself the Director. The budget in 1964 was five million dollars. The announcement gained tremendous space, not only in England, but all over the world, and particularly so in Los

Gandhi's unarmed supporters confront the police guard and submit to a brutal beating without offering any resistance. Although some are killed and many badly maimed by the lathi *blows which rain down on their unresisting bodies, not one attempts to fight back.*

It goes on and on throughout the day with Mirabehn and the other women tending the wounded until they drop with exhaustion.

Angeles. Despite all the niggling problems which still had to be ironed out, Moti and I truly believed we were under way, with a very real hope of going into production on that promised day of 2 October 1965.

Our optimism did not seem misplaced. Early in the new year, together with Jack Rix and John Howell, the Production Designer, and Cameraman Arthur Ibbetson, we left for India. The recce again covered Sabarmati, but this time we also went to Pune to look at the Aga Khan Palace, where Gandhiji, Kasturba and a number of other Indian leaders were imprisoned in 1942.

On our return, we had to face up to the shortcomings in true cinematic terms of Gerry's script. It was still far too long and, although it contained all the primary ingredients, we believed that it now required a really experienced writer in the medium of film to tell this highly complex story in as comprehensible yet tightly disciplined a way as possible. This was a view shared by Joe Levine. Indeed, as far as he was concerned, a new script was an absolute prerequisite. However, everyone felt that Gerry's scholarship and research should not be discarded, and it was therefore decided to engage a second screen writer to work with him. I even went back to Bryan Forbes with a very lucrative offer agreed by Joe Levine, but Bryan felt, as he had initially, that the subject matter really was not for him. This, following some weeks of discussion, came as something of a blow to Joe, I think. Indeed, I am not at all sure that it didn't slightly rock his confidence in the whole project. I certainly detected some reluctance to further

From a public telephone in an Indian village, Walker files his copy on Dharasana—a story that will shock the world. His final indictment, yelled over a crackling telephone line, points the way, inexorably, to the future. 'Whatever moral ascendance the West held was lost today. India is free—for she has taken all that steel and cruelty can give, and she has neither cringed nor retreated.'

127

On location with Martin Sheen.

commitment at that particular time. This was exacerbated when I approached Freddie Raphael and Peter Schaffer and they too turned down the offer. Moti and I also, once again, approached Bob Bolt, but the answer was still no.

Joe was, in addition, very anxious that we should obtain a star name to play Gandhi. Obviously, all the reservations that I had about casting a non-Indian were very much in the forefront of my mind but, nevertheless, I sent the script to several very distinguished British actors. Over the years, sadly, although greatly admiring both the script and the subject matter, Dirk Bogarde, Peter Finch, Albert Finney and Tom Courtenay all, at varying times, declined the offer. In those early days, I have to admit to being fairly certain that one of their causes of concern was my total directorial inexperience. To play a part of the complexity of Gandhi, covering some sixty years, was a daunting prospect for any actor, but to do so under a director without any track record at all could well have been considered foolhardy.

Indiraji came to London in February, partly on government business, but also to see her two sons, Sanjay and Rajiv, who were studying in this country. She brought them both to our home for lunch one Sunday. Even in those days they were obviously very different characters. Both were extremely charming, both intelligent, but the one, Rajiv, reticent almost to the point of shyness, and Sanjay quite the opposite—immensely interested in everything, questioning, often with firm views of his own on a particular subject. They were both greatly interested in the idea of the film, and not a little amused at the prospect of their late grandfather being depicted in it. In years to come, in the late Seventies, I had the opportunity of meeting them again, prior to Sanjay's untimely and tragic death. The assessment of fifteen years beforehand seemed to have been borne out. Sanjay had made a considerable mark on the Indian political scene and, had it not been for the tragedy, might well have become one of the major figures in contemporary Indian history. Rajiv at that time was a pilot for Indian Airlines, retiring but deeply and passionately interested in the subjects that were part of his life. Now, of course, he is a member of the Indian parliament, and in some degree following in his late brother's footsteps, but there is little doubt that, with his high moral standards, he will carve out his own career and follow it in the manner that he alone thinks fit.

The production was running into choppy waters because no major actor appeared to be prepared to commit himself to the film and, more importantly, because we seemed unable to attract a writer of sufficient calibre. It was evident that the production would have to be postponed. With this in view, I felt that I had no alternative—having already given up several possible opportunities of employment—but to accept an offer from Robert Aldrich to play together with Jimmy Stewart, Peter Finch and Hardy Kruger in a film called *The Flight of the Phoenix*. I discussed this situation with Embassy and it was quite clearly agreed between us that, although my absence in America might retard the work on the film, there was no question whatsoever of it being suspended. To my dismay, a letter ultimately came from Embassy stating that because of my absence, the production *was* in fact suspended. Laurence Harbottle replied to the Embassy lawyers, saying that we were both surprised and angered at this move, since it carried with it the cessation of Moti's weekly salary.

I must say here that, judging from the terms in which this particular correspondence was couched, my own feeling was that Joe Levine or Paramount, or both, were getting cold feet. The fact that I was unable to produce a writer of calibre, or an actor of the stature of Alec Guinness, whom I had originally told Joe I hoped would play the part, was going badly against us.

This hiatus was very hard on Moti. He was left in a world with which he was singularly unfamiliar, attempting to keep the ship afloat. I flew to Los Angeles in the third week of April and I was away until the middle of August. The situation was by then a most unhappy one. We appeared to have lost our relationship with Embassy and, through Embassy, with Paramount.

Moti, however, as usual, was indomitable and he made one final assault on Bob Bolt. Bob is a remarkable man, with the highest possible principles, and there was no way in which he would undertake a piece of work unless he felt that he was capable of bringing to it a total conviction. This he declared himself unable to do with this particular subject at this particular time. I do, however, have to say that I believe his refusal was grounded to some extent in the idea of an actor attempting to don the mantle of the director.

6 The prospect of working with yet another of Hollywood's 'living legends' was a stroke of good fortune given to few people whose home is on the other side of the Atlantic. Jimmy Stewart was even taller, if possible, than one could ever have imagined, and I think probably thinner as well. Although he must have been approaching sixty, his youthful figure still conjured up on meeting him images of *Philadelphia Story* and *Mr Smith Goes to Washington*. He and his wife, Gloria, were immensely hospitable to all the actors from overseas, Peter Finch, Hardy Kruger, Ronnie Fraser and Ian Bannen, whom Bob Aldrich had assembled to be amongst the crew or the passengers on the ill-fated *Phoenix*.

The family and I were fortunate enough to be able to live in Gregory Peck's house in Brentwood which, I might add, he allowed us to have rent-free, our only obligation being that of the staff and any work that needed to be done, such as maintaining his rather lovely swimming pool. Nevertheless, despite the novelty of being a resident in Los Angeles and working on what was a fascinating film, my heart remained back in London with Moti. I still suspected that my feelings about Bob Bolt's underlying attitude were not without foundation. I was not particularly surprised, therefore, to receive a letter from Moti asking if I would be prepared, should the necessity arise, to step down as director. What did surprise me was that in the same letter he suggested that I might play the part of Gandhi. Now, no one, no matter how kind, could possibly suggest that I had a sylphlike figure. On the contrary, over the years I have been described variously as 'roly poly', 'tubby hubby', and even just plain fat. But that of course was not the main reason why such a suggestion was untenable.

Despite everything, there was no doubt in my own mind that ideally an Indian should play Gandhi and I think that, in his heart of hearts, this was a view Moti shared. But, that apart, I replied

that I would certainly not stand in the way of the production if
my participation in any form was a deterrent.

Whilst I was in Los Angeles, for some reason I never quite
understood, Moti was very much against my seeing Joe Levine
without his being present. Possibly he believed that Joe was
capable of persuading me in one direction or another, whereas
Moti himself would remain immovable. I did, however, talk to
Joe several times on the phone and the emphasis of the Embassy
reluctance to go forward now appeared to have shifted emphatically from the screen writer to the leading actor. Joe was insistent
that a major star should play the part of Gandhi. As a result of our
failure to reach agreement on this principle, somewhat exasper-
ated, I think, he suggested that Moti and I should look for some
other source of backing. Although there were a number of very
tempting offers to remain in Hollywood, including a leading role

*World opinion forces a change
in the British attitude to India.
Mahatma Gandhi, clad simply in
his* dhoti *and shawl, is invited to
the imposing Viceregal palace in
New Delhi to speak to the
Viceroy, Lord Irwin.*

131

Rehearsing a scene with Steve McQueen for The Sand Pebbles.

in an epic picture with Gregory Peck, I felt I owed it to Moti to return to London and see if we could move the project forward. I arrived back in the middle of August. During my three months' absence, Moti had attempted to interest further screen writers, but without success.

There was now an additional problem for any new backer. Hostilities had broken out between India and Pakistan, and therefore any possibility of a major production in India itself was out of the question.

During my time in Hollywood, I had established a very good rapport with Dick Zanuck, who was the Head of Production for Twentieth Century-Fox and his right-hand man and literary executive, David Brown, who now made me a fascinating offer. Together with the director, Robert Wise, they asked me to play an American sailor in the second lead to Steve McQueen (with whom I had appeared in *The Great Escape*) in their film, *The Sand Pebbles*. This meant going to Taiwan for at least four months. It was a very difficult decision, one of the most complex of my career.

I believed that the probability of mounting *Gandhi* was as elusive at the end of 1965 as it had ever been. Indeed, I was very pessimistic. I felt, however, that my connections within the film industry might be a determining factor in our ultimate ability to raise the ever-mounting sums required to make such a film.

I was very aware that both Moti and his solicitor, Laurence Harbottle, felt that our chances of making progress would be hampered considerably if I was not available. Nevertheless, rightly or wrongly, I accepted the offer to play the part of Frenchie. I

With Jimmy Stewart and Hardy Kruger in The Flight of the Phoenix.

was also very aware that Moti had resigned from the High Commission and was therefore without an income, and that we might well require more money from our own resources to finance a further screenplay.

During this period, being stalled in negotiation with Embassy, Moti and I decided that we would make moves towards Fox, and before I left for Taipei I went to Paris to meet Dick's father, the legendary Darryl Zanuck. As a result, there followed a series of negotiations with him and various executives of Twentieth Century-Fox. They in fact came to nothing, partly because the fighting between India and Pakistan was still continuing, and partly because the Fox board, with the financial failure of *Nine Hours to Rama* in their minds, were very reluctant to invest a large sum of money in what, as far as they were concerned, was a similar kind of project.

I enjoyed my sojourn in Taipei enormously, in no small measure due to Bobby Wise. He was a most kindly and considerate employer and a fascinating film maker to watch exercising his skills. I got to know Steve McQueen really very well and became immensely fond of him. I believe he was underrated as an actor during his lifetime and, had he lived, might well have become one of the Hollywood greats.

I also made two other long-standing friends: Dick Crenna, who played the skipper of the *San Pablo*, and is one of the most amusing and engaging of people, and Candy Bergen, who was making only her second film. She was in her early twenties and as beautiful as any woman I think I have ever met. Although she was somewhat inhibited in her acting, I was sure

133

that she had a considerable talent. However, there was certainly no doubt as to her ability as a photographer. The whole crew, I fear, was forced to listen to my hopes of making the Gandhi film, and even then I asked Candy—all things being equal—if she would play the part of the world-famous Time/Life photographer, Margaret Bourke-White, under whose tuition she studied photography at college. Fifteen years later, she did just that.

I had agreed with Moti before leaving for the Far East that he should have every right to try and set up the picture on his own and that, if he were successful without my involvement, then I would be content to bow out. Taking me at my word, he engaged the American screen writer, Donald Ogden Stewart, and at the beginning of December took him on a trip to India. I felt very strongly that his screenplay, if not actually based on Gerry Hanley's work, should at least take great cognisance of the construction which we had so painstakingly worked out.

While I was in Taipei, Mr Lal Bahandra Shastri suddenly died in Russia, at Tashkent, where he was attempting to bring about a peaceful solution to the India and Pakistan conflict. It was, I suppose, inevitable that the person to succeed him as the third Prime Minister of the Republic of India was Mrs Indira Gandhi. From a purely selfish point of view, this was both good and bad. Good, certainly, in that she would now be in supreme power in New Delhi, but equally a matter of concern, since obviously with her massive new responsibilities neither Moti nor I felt that we had the right to bother her merely about the making of a movie.

During the relatively brief time between shooting in Taipei and moving on to Los Angeles to complete the filming in the studios, I spent a week or two in London, and was able to have a number of meetings with Moti. Ogden Stewart had delivered his screenplay on 31 March. He called it *The Day Gandhi Died*. Although it was well written and had some perceptive sequences in it, it seemed to me that by its desertion of the framework Gerry and I had evolved it failed to bring the story that I personally wished to tell to the screen and I think that, broadly, Moti agreed.

During my time in Hollywood, Jackie Baroda finally withdrew completely from the project. I felt very distressed that I was not with Moti when this disaster occurred, particularly since I had also had talks with United Artists and they, too, had failed to show any real interest. The combination of these factors, and my absence abroad, resulted in a letter from Moti awaiting me on my return in August. He felt we really had to re-think our attitudes

134

Dawn in New Delhi and the temperature is near freezing as the crew film Ben Kingsley climbing the steps of the Presidential palace, formerly the Viceroy's official residence.

and programme, and that unless I was prepared to devote myself one hundred per cent to *Gandhi*, forgoing any other engagements whatsoever, each of us should have the right, always in the name of Indo-British Films, to proceed separately and only come together in order to conclude a deal.

I felt it was impossible for me to give the categoric assurance Moti required, and therefore had to agree to his making any independent moves he wished. I believed I still had hopes of backing from Twentieth Century-Fox in that while I was in Los Angeles Dick Zanuck and David Brown had asked me to direct a picture, which would have been my first directorial assignment. It was called *Choice Cuts*, a very bizarre thriller, which I read and just did not like at all. So, although it might have provided a track record, making me more acceptable as the director of *Gandhi*, I decided after careful consideration that I must decline. Nevertheless, when they later asked me to make a guest appearance in *Dr Dolittle*, it seemed a further opportunity to maintain my connection with Fox, and I returned to Los Angeles later in the year. It was the one and only time that I have played in a musical, and I owe whatever success I had to Leslie Bricusse for having had the wild idea, to Dick Fleischer for being prepared to direct me, but perhaps most of all to the movie's choreographer, Herbie Ross, and his wife, Nora Kaye. They were enchantingly biased in their faith that somehow or other I could get away with it.

Moti had maintained a close relationship with Bob Bolt, who now said he would write the screenplay, provided he had the right to approve the director. My understanding was that originally the director was to be David Lean, but somehow or another, neither Bob nor Moti were able to pin him down. Bob's play, *A Man For All Seasons*, was being filmed at that time, directed by Fred Zinnemann, and Bob suggested to Moti that he should come to the studios and meet him. The result was that Fred said he would like to undertake the Gandhi film on completion of *A Man For All Seasons*. Moti told me of this development, and asked me to back down in order to permit Fred to direct. This I did straight away, and wrote to Moti: 'Zinnemann is a truly great director, one of the best in the world, and if I have to relinquish my dream, well, I could hardly hope to imagine a better person to whom I could pass it on.' They both very kindly suggested that when the film was eventually made I might like to play one of the principal supporting parts.

It was terrible after this length of time to feel that I would no longer be part of setting up the project. One small comfort was the calibre of those involved and the fact that, due to my recent work as an actor, I was able to pay Moti an allowance sufficient to keep him going—as I did on a number of other occasions. Through Bob Bolt a major interest was created with MGM and he and Moti spent some weeks in India, allowing Bob to do the sort of research that he required before setting about such a major task. In the end, for reasons which were never fully explained to me, Fred Zinnemann withdrew, and it was David Lean who, once again, became the most likely director.

Although David was now showing great interest, I felt dubious about his ultimate involvement. Some years beforehand, I had flown to Madrid to visit him, to make certain that the interest he had previously shown in the project was no impediment to my going ahead. He had assured me categorically that he would never wish to make the Gandhi film; it had been one of his ambitions, but it was no longer, and that decision was irrevocable. My purpose in going to see him then had been that, if there really was a chance of this master of the cinema making this particular subject, it should be in his hands rather than in mine.

As I understand it, towards the end of 1967, quite out of the blue, Bob suddenly announced to Moti that, prior to making *Gandhi*, he and David wished to make 'a little film', which of course would delay *Gandhi* for a short time. Moti, I know, was shattered, but of course there was nothing he could do about it, and he simply had to await developments. The 'little film' that they referred to turned out to be *Ryan's Daughter* which took three years before it was ready to be premièred. Nevertheless, Moti was somewhat encouraged by the appearance on the scene of David's producer, Anthony Havelock-Allan, and I must say, knowing him as the producer of *In Which We Serve*, I too felt that I must be wrong in my assessment of David's interests, and that there was now a real desire on their part to make *Gandhi*. This view was further confirmed when I learnt that Moti was to take Tony to India. Certainly Bob gave Moti every reason to believe that things were now really going forward when he wrote, the film 'is as secure as any project can be until the opening night'. However,

Despite his protectionist attitude towards imported cloth which has caused hardship in British mills, Gandhi is feted by cotton workers during a brief visit to Lancashire.

despite all the optimism, no satisfactory documents were forth-coming from Metro, and Moti was still left with only hope to keep his spirits alive. He threw all his energies into the Gandhi centenary celebrations, and indeed was probably as responsible as anyone in England for their undoubted success.

Although Moti did his best to keep me abreast of develop-ments, during the latter part of 1966 and throughout 1967 I felt very cut off. I played in *The Bliss of Mrs Blossom* with Jimmy Booth and a miraculous, unique comedienne, Shirley MacLaine. I also renewed my relationship with Basil Dearden, who was directing a film with David Hemmings called *Only When I Larf*, based on a novel by Len Deighton. Len and Brian Duffy were the producers, and thereby, as they say, hangs a tale.

One day in the summer of 1967, Johnny Mills rang me and said he had a screenplay on which he'd been working with Len. It was a film version of Joan Littlewood's brilliant *Oh! What a Lovely War*. I have to admit to thinking that he must be dotty, for I could not conceive anything which was more theatrical in concept. It seemed to me that it was not only ludicrous, but quite impossible, to transfer it into film terms. Naturally, I didn't say so on the phone, but I did ask why Johnny wanted me to read it. 'Len and I thought perhaps you might like to direct,' he said. I was utterly bowled over. It seemed that I was back in 1963 where I had started with *Gandhi*. I couldn't understand why anybody, now that I had failed to mount the Gandhi film, should be prepared to consider me as a director and, what was more, the director of a musical.

The script was delivered that night, and I started reading it about eleven o'clock. I rang Johnny the following morning and told him that, in my opinion, the adaptation which Len had devised was a stroke of genius. With the new setting of the story, it worked as if it had been originally conceived for the cinema. I said I would adore to direct it, but had to admit that I was puzzled why they had chosen me. He replied that in discussing the project they had both agreed that the picture needed a 'new eye', some-one who was prepared to try things which perhaps had not been done in quite that way before. Johnny had told Len of my passionate desire to direct *Gandhi*, and they had agreed that he should ask me to read the script.

Without doubt the fact that I directed *Oh! What a Lovely War* and subsequently four other movies is in no small measure due to Johnny Mills. He has been the most marvellous friend and with-

Accompanied by Mirabehn and Charlie Andrews, Gandhi walks through the rain in London's East End.

Gandhi shakes hands with Prime Minister Ramsay MacDonald (Terrence Hardiman) outside No. 10 Downing Street in London, masking his profound disappointment that the All-Government Conference of 1931, has failed to advance the cause of Indian Independence.

out his faith in me, *Oh! What a Lovely War* would never have happened, and consequently none of the other films.

However, despite the fact that there was a screenplay, and Johnny himself was to play Field-Marshal Haig, and Len and Brian Duffy were to produce and I direct, no funds had been raised. Johnny Redway wanted me to go to Paramount. Bud Ornstein was their Chief Executive in the United Kingdom, and after he had read the screenplay, I went to see him.

He was greatly encouraging. Paramount, he said, had just been taken over by a remarkable man called Charles Bludhorn. Charlie was a true entrepreneur, and Bud thought by far the best way of persuading the company to back a project which was as off beat as *Oh! What a Lovely War* was for me to have the opportunity of selling the idea to him. He was due in London very shortly, and so, four days before I started shooting on *The Bliss of Mrs Blossom*, I went to the Dorchester Hotel to meet him.

I have done a number of auditions in my life, but never one which had such far-reaching results in terms of my career. Fortunately I knew practically every number from the show. I sang, half-danced and acted eight or ten different sequences for Charlie and his Chief Executive, Martin Davies. Charlie seemed captivated with my description of how these marvellous numbers could be conveyed in terms of cinema, although I don't think for one moment he felt that the movie could be a financial bonanza. On the other hand, he was a European who had only relatively recently gone to the United States, and his knowledge of the First World War and the European sense of humour and satire was very real. He had always been a great gambler in business terms, and therefore seemed susceptible to this particular risk.

The one tricky question he asked me was what sort of cast I could assemble. Throwing caution to the wind, and counting on the *esprit de corps* of actors and actresses, I reeled off a mammoth list of names: Laurence Olivier, Ralph Richardson, Alec Guinness, John Gielgud, Michael Redgrave, Vanessa Redgrave, Jack Hawkins, Dirk Bogarde, Phyllis Calvert, Kenneth More, Peter O'Toole, John Clements, Albert Finney, Susannah York, Maggie Smith and, of course, Johnny Mills.

Charlie with, I believe, a fair amount of scepticism, said, 'Dickie, if you can get just six of those names, you have the finance you need.' In the event, thirteen appeared in the film.

Following the completion of *The Bliss of Mrs Blossom* and *Only When I Larf*, Len, Duffy and a colleague of theirs, Pat

Tilley, and I started serious work to prepare *Oh! What a Lovely War* for the screen. Mike Stanley-Evans who had some years before joined Indo-British Films with a view to being the Executive Producer on *Gandhi*, in which he had always had such faith, was to co-produce. This was a friendship and a business relationship which proved to be of inestimable value to me on *Lovely War, Young Winston, A Bridge Too Far*, and finally *Gandhi*.

Having boasted somewhat rashly about my ability to produce a host of world-famous names, I had to do something about it. The first person I went to see was Sir Laurence Olivier, and Larry's reaction to my story and resultant request was typical. He loved the idea of an actor directing a movie. He had always believed in the concept of actor-managership in the theatre, and he saw no reason why it should not be extended to the cinema. He not only said that he would play any part in the film, even if it was merely a walk-on, but he would appear on a minimal daily rate salary which he would allow me to quote to the other stars I was about to approach. The great man's generosity was the key which finally opened the door for my venture into direction.

We started shooting *Oh! What a Lovely War* on 27 March, and finished on Saturday, 24 August. I don't think I have ever worked so hard in my life, and I don't think I've ever felt so tired as I did on Sunday the 25th.

These periods are pretty hard on one's family. One adopts a sort of monastic existence—working, eating, sleeping and working. Without Sheila's love and understanding I would never have made *Lovely War* or, for that matter, the other films I have directed. Much of whatever credit I have reaped is hers by rights.

The 1931 Conference in London. An archive photograph.

At the outbreak of the Second World War, Gandhi arrives at Bombay Station, intending to make a pacifist speech. As always on his journeys now, the Indian people crowd forward just to catch a glimpse of their beloved Mahatma.

In varying states of preparedness, *Lovely War* was shown to a number of people, and the general consensus of opinion seemed favourable. Amongst those to see it early in 1969 was Joe Levine. It had its première in London on 10 April and received I suppose the best set of notices that I have ever had in my life. The business in the United Kingdom was phenomenal, but sadly not so in the rest of the world, although in America the reviews were almost as good as those in London. I felt, therefore, that there really was an infinitely greater chance now of raising funds for *Gandhi*. However, at this particular time I had abdicated my right to the film, in favour of Moti, Bob Bolt and Fred Zinnemann or David Lean.

My salary for *Oh! What a Lovely War* had been a fairly nominal one, and so I had to replenish the coffers by playing in several films, including *A Severed Head*, *Loot*, and a guest appearance with my beloved Larry in *David Copperfield*.

In September 1969 Moti suffered a second heart attack, and was immediately rushed into intensive care in a hospital in Hampstead. I found myself in a rather difficult position. Due to the critical success of *Oh! What a Lovely War* and Joe Levine's personal admiration for it, he was prepared once again to discuss his involvement with *Gandhi*. Because I still had grave doubts at the back of my mind as to whether Bob and either David or Fred would in fact make *Gandhi*, I decided to go and see Joe. I talked the matter over with Dorothy Kothari while Moti was still in hospital. I obviously did not wish to give him concern, but equally it seemed to me that, if the project fell through as far as Bolt was concerned, then nothing could be more conducive to Moti's recovery than the thought that there was another string to our bow.

Moti left hospital in the middle of October, and I told him of my wish to open negotiations once more with Joe. He replied that there was no possible way in which he could abandon the Bolt/Lean set-up and that, if I wished to discuss the matter with Levine, I must do so on my own initiative. In the knowledge that there were still no documents signed with MGM, I told Moti in December that I was going to New York to see Joe.

During the last fortnight of 1969 there had been a number of theatrical celebrations in London to honour Sir Noël Coward, who was celebrating his seventieth birthday. Sheila and I saw quite a lot of him at that time and went to stay with him at his home in Switzerland early in the New Year. The day after we

returned, on 15 January, Moti died. During the preceding two or three years I had, to an extent, lost the closeness of my relationship with him. It was a matter of considerable sadness, but I suppose in the light of his new association with those who seemed most likely to be able to bring his dream to fruition, it was inevitable. I had been to see him several times in hospital in the latter part of 1969, and had received, as usual, the most enchanting letters from him. But now, suddenly, he was no more.

And neither was Louis Fischer, who died on the same day in New Jersey.

As far as *Gandhi* was concerned, I was of course powerless. With Moti gone, I had to respect his last wishes, that the initiative

On his return from England, Gandhi confers with Indian leaders at the ashram. Although the All-Government Conference in London did not prove an important step towards Independence, as he had hoped, Gandhi assures the others that it will not now be long in coming. Those present (left to right) are Pyarelal Nayar (Pankaj Mohan), Patel, Azad, Nehru and Kripalani (Anang Desai).

Married, in The Bliss of Mrs Blossom, *to that miraculous unique comedienne, Shirley MacLaine.*

BELOW
At the end of Brighton Pier where we filmed Oh! What a Lovely War.

BELOW RIGHT
Laurence Olivier practises dance steps for Oh! What a Lovely War, *watched by Johnny Mills.*

for making the film should reside with Bob Bolt and, supposedly, David Lean.

Of one thing, however, I was absolutely certain. In 1963 Moti and I had together determined to make the film. The inspiration emanated from Moti, and I resolved that if ever again the opportunity arose for me to assume the task of bringing Gandhi's words and love to the world, nothing would give me a greater sense of fulfilment or indeed a better opportunity of perpetuating the name of Motilal Kothari.

1970 was a strange year. I missed Moti very much and I felt
completely cut off from *Gandhi*. Bob Bolt was, I am sure, aware
of my isolation and in March sent me a copy of his script outline,
called *Gandhiji*. This treatment had some wonderful passages,
but I still felt that it did not improve upon the construction Gerry
Hanley and I had previously evolved. Reading Bob's outline was
tantalising, because I was fully aware that I personally had no
right to pursue the subject.

To allay this feeling and to earn some money, it was vital to find
work. An interesting subject to direct came into my hands
through a producer named Kurt Unger. Entitled *Pope Joan*, it
was about a medieval belief that one particular Pope was actually
a woman. What really intrigued me, though, was the quality of
the script. The writer was an American who had lived in England
for many years, and his name was Jack Briley. Unfortunately, I
came to a creative impasse with Mr Unger and we parted company. However, I did decide that one day, if the opportunity ever
arose, I would try to work with Jack Briley.

Around this time, Carl Foreman asked me to lunch and made a
most tempting offer. For a number of years, he had wanted to
make a film based on the early years of Winston Churchill. He
had written a first draft screenplay, and would produce the film
for his own company. Having seen *Oh! What a Lovely War*, Carl
asked me not only to play the part of Lord Randolph but also to
direct the film. I was very flattered. However, the more I thought
about it, the more I realised that to undertake both playing and
directing would be foolhardy. When finally I asked Carl if he
would be content for me merely to direct, he willingly agreed.

His screenplay was in an early form and needed at least six
months' work before we could move on to the next stage of
production. He accepted that we should wait until I could read
the final version, in order to be sure I had the confidence to
embark on this enormous project. I felt that if I were to pull off

7

British officers await Gandhi on Bombay station. Eliciting the information that he intends to condemn the war recently started in Europe, they put him under armed arrest. Having stated that she will speak in his place, Kasturba is also taken into custody, together with Mirabehn.

Young Winston it could but enhance my chances of directing *Gandhi* since, at the back of my mind, I must admit, was an inkling Bob might eventually find that David Lean would withdraw. In this assessment, though, I was somewhat premature.

In the midst of doing research for *Young Winston*, a most intriguing acting offer came my way. It's difficult to describe Leslie Linder. As Johnny Redway's ex-partner, he was an agent, and he was also a restaurateur: at the same time he was an impresario, a film producer, a keep-fit fiend, and a man bursting with creative ideas. He had read Ludovic Kennedy's book, *Ten Rillington Place*, and asked if I would like to play the pathetic,

homicidal necrophiliac, John Reginald Christie. The 'hawks'
were out again, mounting an emotive campaign to re-introduce
capital punishment. Being resolutely opposed to the death penal-
ty, I felt that steeping myself in this particular character, however
unpleasant, would be worthwhile if, as a result, people were
persuaded that hanging was not only barbaric but also could
cause irretrievable miscarriages of justice. Timothy Evans,
Christie's young Welsh lodger, had been hanged for the murder
of his wife. After his death on the gallows, and the discovery of
Christie's mass killings, many believed that Evans should never
have been brought to trial.

147

Standing in the actual doorway of No. 10 Rillington Place, home of the mass murderer, John Reginald Christie. The house has since been demolished.

Richard Fleischer, for whom I'd worked on *Dr Dolittle*, was to be the director. Timothy Evans's wife was to be played by Judy Geeson and Evans himself by the brilliant young English actor, John Hurt. For me, living daily as Christie for the five weeks it took to shoot the film, was deeply disturbing, but in the long term not unrewarding.

My work with Carl Foreman continued throughout the next few months, and I was becoming more and more intrigued with *Young Winston*. A day or so before he and I left for Marakesh to look for locations, my brothers Dave and John and I took part in a ceremony commemorating the Governor's tenure at Leicester University. The new arts building was to be named after him. Johnny declared it open, and Dave and I were given honorary degrees.

Before finally agreeing to direct *Young Winston*, I had to make a very difficult decision. After long talks, Laurence Olivier had asked me if I would become his associate director at the National Theatre. It would have been a fundamental change for me, and certainly would mean my having to give up *Gandhi* for ever. Despite the unique nature of the offer and the joy of working with Larry, I suppose it was the prospect of abandoning *Gandhi* that made me decline. In October, Carl announced *Young Winston* and that I was to direct it.

After making several trips to New York, I was finally able to persuade Annie Bancroft to play Winston's mother, having been determined that she should accept the part. She was, and still is in my judgement, one of the finest screen actresses in the world and proved to be perfectly cast. Carl and I agreed that Robert Shaw would be a wonderful Randolph, but the question of Winston was much more complex. We saw innumerable young actors and screen-tested four of them. I don't think Carl shared my initial certainty that Simon Ward would give a miraculous performance but, as it turned out, that is exactly what he did.

The picture was not the success it should have been, although it was received with considerable acclaim when it opened in London. I must of course bear a large part of the blame—certainly it was not the fault of the players. Carl and I never saw totally eye to eye, either on the script or in the picture's editing, and I think that the finished film suffered in consequence.

Gandhi languished somewhat. Bob Bolt seemed unable to pin David Lean down, and, consequently, wrote and directed his own first film, *Lady Caroline Lamb*.

148

Winston Churchill, MP, and his wife visit us on location and meet Simon Ward, playing his famous grandfather.

In the spring of 1972, when I had completed my work on *Young Winston*, Bob Bolt suggested we should meet. At last he had given up hope of ever persuading David to make a firm commitment and now declared that if I could raise the finance he would be content for me to direct *Gandhi*.

Bob's new attitude prompted me to approach Joe Levine to see if, with further experience under my belt and a potential screenplay by Bolt, he might once again be interested. This proved to be so, and I made several trips to New York. Joe was now the president of Avco Embassy Pictures and therefore his own master. He seemed thrilled that a writer of Bob's eminence was prepared to commit himself to the production, and we drew up preliminary agreements under which Joe and I were to co-produce the picture and I was to direct. My excitement at being involved again was boundless, and I remember exchanging a series of euphoric telegrams with Joe, conveying the bubbling enthusiasm that I felt at starting work with Bob Bolt. Bob and I spent a great deal of time together, planning the film sequence by sequence. This manner of working was very productive, and the whole of the Southern African segment in the script worked out very smoothly. On my many trips to the States I was entertained most royally by Joe and his wife Rosalie, out in Connecticut. They have a magnificent house, every wall adorned with a plethora of Impressionist paintings, in addition to an extraordinary collection of Andrew Wyeths. We would also go out on his yacht and, standing together on the bridge, dream aloud about the Gandhi film. I am convinced that Joe, at that particular time, had every intention of making it.

I received a letter from him, I remember, in March 1973, which

With Anne Bancroft in her role as Churchill's mother in Young Winston.

During the Second World War, the British imprison Gandhi in the Aga Khan Palace at Pune. There, he continues to fulfil his daily quota of spinning whilst meditating on India's future.

ended: 'I do want to tell you that the more I think of our project, the more I love it, and I know it can do us both (especially you) much credit. I, of course, as you know, will take all the bows. Love Joe.'

It was at about this time that we agreed to approach two world-famous artists in the hope that they might be involved in the picture. The first was Ravi Shankar. He expressed enormous interest and said that once we could give him a precise timetable, he would be delighted to write the music. The second approach —an idea of mine—was made to Picasso. I knew his potter, Madame Susanne Ramié, in the Riviera town of Vallauris, and she kindly asked him if, in principle, he would consider designing our logo and main advertising graphic. Almost unbelievably, we received a message that he appeared willing.

The Governor, who had been living with Sheila and me for some time, died in March 1973. He was tremendously excited by the prospect of our going into production, and knowing that Ravi Shankar and Picasso might be involved thrilled him immeasurably. I was deeply happy that we had this news before he died.

In April I took the decision—momentous as far as the production was concerned—of assigning the rights in all that Indo-British Films possessed to Avco Embassy. They committed themselves to finance *Gandhi* with a budget limit of $6 million. Accompanying the assignment went confirmation of Bob Bolt's engagement as screen writer. I received his first draft at the end of April. It was, inevitably, almost an hour over length. We agreed that there were several aspects which needed to be sharpened up but that, in making any cuts, we must allow for other areas which needed expanding.

In July I left for another major recce trip to India, and was there for approximately three weeks. Accompanied by Vala Kothari and Mike Stanley-Evans, who was taking control of the production side, we again went to Pune, and also to Dandi beach, Simla and Amritsar, ending up at Ahmedabad. Shortly after our return, Bob's script was finally sent to Joe.

He was not excited about it. Indeed, it resulted in a somewhat acrimonious correspondence between them. We had hoped that we would start shooting in January 1974. However, very firm instructions arrived from Avco Embassy's lawyers, informing me not to engage any personnel whatsoever until Mr Levine's formal approval of the final script had been given.

Margaret Bourke-White (Candice Bergen), the famous Life *magazine photo-journalist, with Mahatma Gandhi at the Aga Khan Palace at Pune. Gandhi initiates her into the complexities of spinning. Happiness, he explains, does not come with things – even twentieth-century things – but it can come from work and pride in what you do.*

With Ben Kingsley at Pune.

Under the principal terms agreed with Avco Embassy in 1973, I was now drawing an overhead fee which broadly covered my office expenditure, but in no way provided me with a normal income. However, in October 1973 the payments ceased quite arbitrarily. I had a brief conversation with Joe on the phone, in which he said that he was experiencing considerable difficulties in raising the finance for the film, because India had formally announced her alignment with the Arab countries in the Middle East war. Joe, of course, was Jewish.

This created a problem. If the production was not to proceed, and since I had earned no money for some time, I would have to accept one of the offers that I was being made as an actor. Inevitably, this would result in further delay.

Finally, on 29 November, I received a letter from Joe, which read, 'The political factors and the financial complications in connection with *Gandhi* compel me to advise you that unfortunately it is not possible to make any plans at this time to proceed with the production of this picture. I am not happy that circumstances have forced me to make this decision, as I remain convinced that *Gandhi* would be one of the greatest pictures ever made. Yours, Joe.'

Bob Bolt was very angry, and wrote Joe several forthright letters, saying that he felt badly let down, having received assurances from Joe before he started work on the screenplay that the funds for making *Gandhi* were not only available but secured.

The outcome of this latest correspondence with Joe and Avco Embassy was that, yet again, he suggested we should look elsewhere for finance. I wrote saying that, should we be successful, I would of course wish to exercise my 'buy back' rights.

In the interim, I had managed to accomplish a number of things. One was to meet Madeleine Slade—Mirabehn, as Gandhi called her.

Back in 1965, Moti and I had attempted to visit her at her home just outside Vienna. We arrived by plane to find that the snowbound roads were impassable for some days. Unfortunately, because of other commitments, I had to return to London, but Moti did manage to see her, and she was fascinated by the prospect of our film. However, I determined in 1973 that I really must try and pay her a visit.

She lived in a little cottage on the edge of the Vienna Woods. As the car drew up, she came out of the door: amazingly tall, still very upright, with grey swept-back hair and a large pair of thick glasses. Well wrapped in heavy woollies, she strode down the path with her arms spread out in greeting, while standing discreetly in the background was Datt, her devoted Indian bearer.

We quickly developed a warm relationship, and she began to relate anecdote after anecdote. Provided it spread the true spirit of Gandhi, she believed the film was a wonderful idea. I asked her a thousand questions; but one reply I remember most clearly of all. I said, 'Mirabehn, do you believe there is a particular quality that the actor who is to play Gandhiji must have?'

She paused for a moment and then, in that marvellous husky voice with her face breaking into a beaming smile, she replied, 'He must be very good.'

My time with her was all too brief. However, I did see her again, twice in Vienna and on a number of occasions when, for two years, she decided to return to England and stayed in Tunbridge Wells. She was enormously generous. She not only passed on to me the majority of the letters Gandhi had written her, which I undertook ultimately to lodge with one of the official archives, but also her own copy of his autobiography which he himself had given her many years before.

Mira's encouragement was unstinting, particularly during the period of Morarji Desai's Prime Ministership when Indira Gandhi was out of office, and she wrote urging him to endorse Pandit Nehru's original approval of the film. We sent her photographs from *Gandhi* at the end of the shooting and, thanking us,

Mirabehn shows me the copy of Gandhi's autobiography which he gave to her and she, in turn, at this meeting presented to me.

she expressed her delight in their veracity, although she complained bitterly that Geraldine James, who portrayed her, was so very much more beautiful than herself.

Almost more than anyone, I wanted her to see the finished result. Sadly, two or three months before her ninetieth birthday, on 20 July 1982, as I was writing this chapter, she died. I grieve for her greatly.

In recalling 1973, I must also mention Capital Radio. Shortly after I returned from the location work on *Young Winston*, colleagues asked me to become chairman of a company we had previously formed which was to apply for the franchise for the entertainment station in London. Almost unbelievably, since we were by no means the most powerful consortium, our group was selected. Time was not, however, on our side and at 4.15 a.m. on the morning of 5 October, with only forty-five minutes to go before we went on the air for the first time, I was feverishly vacuuming the studios. Having introduced the station to London at 5.00 a.m., I joined the Managing Director John Whitney and a mass of friends and colleagues for a feast of bangers and mash cooked on braziers on the concrete floor of the foyer. Subsequently, John was appointed Director General of the IBA and I shall miss him greatly, although he will remain a

Talking with Margaret Bourke-White, Kasturba explains Gandhi's attitude towards the liberation of women. Her husband, she says, has always recognised that there are two kinds of slavery in India – one for women and one for Untouchables. Mirabehn agrees that Gandhi has always fought against both.

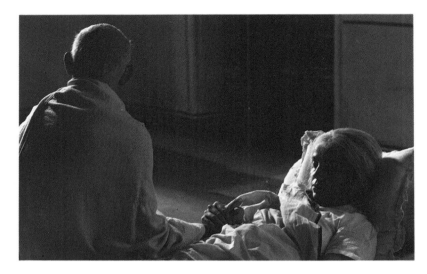

Imprisoned with Gandhi at the Aga Khan Palace, Kasturba suffers a massive heart attack and dies.

life-long friend.

Capital was a great stimulus to my morale. It did not, however, assist my bank balance. Not to put too fine a point on it, I was flat broke. My last salary had come from *Young Winston* some two years beforehand.

As soon as possible, therefore, I simply had to earn some money. There are always plenty of tempting offers when you are unable to accept them — when in fact you need one desperately, they are few and far between. However, in February 1974 I left for Isfahan in Iran to appear in yet another version of Agatha Christie's *Ten Little Indians*, this time under the title of *Then There Were None*. The film itself was pretty dreadful; nevertheless, the salary that I received allowed me to pay off my debts, reduce my overdraft to more reasonable proportions and keep going for a further few months.

In the spring of 1974 my financial straits were further eased when I was offered the co-starring part in a film entitled *Brannigan*, directed by Douglas Hickox and starring John Wayne. It was the only film that 'Duke' ever made in England, and it was all shot in and around London. I remember *Brannigan* with some amusement because it contained one scene in which ostensibly I laid 'Duke' Wayne low with a right-hander to his chin!

It was followed by a relatively brief appearance in Michael Anderson's film, *Conduct Unbecoming*.

Towards the end of the year, *Gandhi* talks were taking place with Warner Brothers. Thus I found myself staying at the Beverly

Hills Hotel in Los Angeles during the last week of February. On returning from a meeting with Frank Wells, the President of Warner Brothers, I was handed a note which read, 'What the hell are you doing here, come up and see me. Love, Joe.' Joe, of course, was Joe Levine. He had some months previously severed his connection with Avco Embassy and was now an independent producer.

I went up to the palatial suite the Levines always occupy. His wife, Rosalie, was with him. On the long, glass coffee table was a hardcover copy of Cornelius Ryan's book, *A Bridge Too Far*, the Second World War story of the battle of Arnhem. It caught my eye the moment I went in, since Joe had sent it to me to read some months previously. He greeted me as if we had only seen each other a few days beforehand. I told him that I was at last about to sign a deal for *Gandhi* and that I would be asking Avco to assign the rights back to my company.

In reply, Joe growled in his normal speaking voice—as if addressing a capacity crowd at Madison Square Garden—'Why the hell don't you give up that goddam B-movie and do something worthwhile with me?'

'I can't,' I replied, 'I'm going to make *Gandhi*.'

'You'll never make that goddam film, not without me.'

'I will, Joe, I'm going to sign a deal with Warner Brothers.'

'I'll tell you what,' he said, 'if you don't get the goddam contract, why don't you direct *A Bridge Too Far*?'

I was amazed, knowing that this was no flippant remark. Joe was making me a firm offer. It was an extraordinary thing to do on his part. In the first place, I had only directed two films and, moreover, I knew that there were at least half a dozen top directors in Hollywood, all desperately anxious to make *A Bridge Too Far*. But, in a way, the offer was typical of Joe. If he felt instinctively that somebody was right for a particular project, convention or cowardice would never deter him. I had read the book and found it a most exciting and revealing work of its genre.

But I told Joe I was convinced that, unless something totally unexpected happened, my contract with Warner Brothers would go through. He pressed me, asking if I would do *A Bridge Too Far* should the deal, for any reason, collapse. And, on the spur of the moment, I agreed.

As things turned out, the totally unexpected did happen. There was a major faction which opposed *Gandhi* at Warner Brothers and the deal was called off.

156

Joe came straight over to Europe and, with his Production Designer, Terry Marsh, we started combing Holland for the location we required. Being with Joe was, as usual, highly stimulating. He was a great enthusiast, and was again earnestly talking of *Gandhi* being our next project together.

The pre-production period for *A Bridge Too Far* was twelve months, and it was certainly not too long. The mounting of a film on that scale, costing some $25 million, assembling all the hardware, aircraft, tanks, artillery and organising the massive construction programme required was a phenomenal undertaking.

In addition, Joe was determined to make it an all-star cast, with leading players from Europe, Great Britain and America. We both believed that in portraying the almost larger than life figures who participated in the real battle of Arnhem, it was necessary to cast the parts with the biggest possible names, particularly since they would be making relatively brief appearances. We ended up with an exciting a line-up as had been assembled within the last decade or so: Dirk Bogarde, James Cann, Michael Caine, Sean Connery, Edward Fox, Elliott Gould, Gene Hackman, Anthony Hopkins, Hardy Kruger, Laurence Olivier, Ryan O'Neal, Robert Redford, Maximilian Schell and Liv Ullmann.

However, the most formidable task was that undertaken by the screen writer, gathering into a coherent shape the highly complex strands of activity; involving the whole action from the point of

Filming A Bridge Too Far *with Joe Levine in Deventer, Holland. In the background is the bridge we used to simulate the original at nearby Arnhem which was blown up at the end of one of World War Two's hardest fought battles.*

view of the British, the Americans, the Poles and the Dutch. The assignment was given to William Goldman. Joe arranged for me to meet him in New York. He was very shy, a man of few words, really, until you got to know him. He is an avid sports fan, and one of the most knowledgeable wine connoisseurs I have ever met. Through that, he, his wife Ilene and I had an immediate *rapport*. Bill taught me a great deal about the disciplines of screen-writing, and he finally delivered, in my opinion, an exceptional script which, more than any other single contribution to the team effort, made *A Bridge Too Far* work as a movie.

Joe displayed great generosity to me. He paid me very well, gave me ten per cent of the net profits and, half-way through the schedule, having seen the first assembly of six weeks' work, increased my salary. He never once interfered with my decisions in relation to the shooting of the film, or to its editing. Equally, he kept a meticulous eye on the production affairs.

2 January 1976 was a memorable day in that my name appeared in the New Year's Honours List. A few weeks later, as Vice-President of the British Academy of Film and Television Arts, I was one of those who received Her Majesty the Queen when she opened our new premises in Piccadilly. Joe and Rosalie were among the guests, since he was one of the Academy's benefactors.

After the formal opening, the Queen admired the gold replica of Arnhem bridge adorning the handle of Joe's walking stick. As luck would have it, a photographer who had been dogging Her Majesty's heels was for some unaccountable reason not now in evidence. After learning the relevance of the cane, Her Majesty wished Joe good fortune with the film and moved on.

'Where's that goddam lousy photographer?' said Joe, between clenched teeth. 'Of all the goddam lousy stinking pictures he's ever taken, there was a great one. Me, the bridge, and the Queen of England in the same picture. What a memento for the kids. I'll kill the bastard!'

Joe had wanted that picture very badly.

Shooting on *A Bridge Too Far* began on 26 April, and ended on 6 October. I remember being exhausted on completing *Oh! What a Lovely War*, but if possible I felt even more tired at the end of *Bridge*. It had been a remarkable experience and I had been very fortunate in those who had been involved in it with me. The cast apart, Mike Stanley-Evans of course was acting as Executive Producer, and the production team of John Palmer, Eric Rattray and Terry Clegg were of invaluable help. Terry Marsh and Stuart Craig headed the Art Department, with Michael White as Sketch Artist, Simon Kaye was the Sound Recordist, David Tomblin as

LEFT
Lord Louis Mountbatten (Peter Harlowe), last Viceroy of India, will preside over the transition from British rule to Independence. He and Lady Louis (Jane Myerson) are greeted by Nehru and other dignitaries on their arrival in Delhi.

RIGHT
Talks on the formula for India's Independence are under way in Delhi. To Gandhi's despair, Jinnah is determined that the country shall be partitioned into separate Hindu and Muslim states. Nehru reminds him that people of both religions live side by side throughout the sub-continent.

the First Assistant, Norton Knatchbull the Location Manager, and Tony Gibbs the Editor. The Casting Director, probably the best I have ever known, was Miriam Brickman, who was at RADA with Sheila and me. The Cameraman was Geoff Unsworth, whose Operator was Peter MacDonald. Many of them went on to work with me on *Gandhi*. Sadly, both Miriam and Geoff died before we started but, if they had lived, I know they would have wished to be part of the crew.

Having completed the editing and dubbing with a marvellous score by Jock Addison, I showed the film in its final shape to Joe, and he formally delivered it to United Artists.

About a month later I left for Calcutta, to make a guest appearance in *The Chess Players*, the first film that Satyajit Ray made in Hindi and in colour. Some months before, he had had lunch with me in London, and asked me to play the part of General Outram. Without hesitation I told him that I would be absolutely delighted.

'But ought you not to see the script?' he asked.

I replied that if he asked me to read the telephone directory, I would agree. It was the first time that I had ever been to Calcutta. Manikda, as he is known by his crew, and his producer, Suresh Jindal, met me at the airport. I was carrying my entire costume with me, and started shooting the day after my arrival.

I have never been so hot in my life. I was wearing a scarlet dress uniform, buttoned up to the neck. The studios had no air-conditioning, and the temperature was around 140°F: indeed, there were several moments when I thought I would pass out.

Filming The Chess Players *in Calcutta with Satyajit Ray.*

Ray is a meticulous film maker, unique in the number of functions that he performs. He writes, designs the production, acts as his own set dresser, operates the camera, composes the music, edits, and of course directs. The result is that in the end the film is truly a creation of Satyajit Ray. I not only enjoyed playing in the picture, but I count working for him as one of the milestones in my acting career.

I returned to London, setting off a day or so later for the opening of *A Bridge Too Far* in Tokyo, to be followed by Ohio, Boston, New York, Washington, Deventer—the little town in Holland where we shot the picture—Amsterdam and finally, on 23 June, London. The guests of honour at the London opening were the Duchess of Kent and Lord Louis, who was again inquiring about progress on the Gandhi film. I had to explain that nothing had been done to further its production for some two

years, but now that *A Bridge Too Far* was completed, I very much hoped Joe Levine would agree to finance it.

However, there was to be yet another postponement. Bill Goldman had written the screenplay for his own novel, *Magic*, and Joe had acquired the rights. It was an essentially American story, intimate, with just four principal characters, and both Bill and Joe very much wanted me to direct it. I agreed ultimately, again on the very firm promise volunteered by Joe that on its completion we really would embark on *Gandhi*. Indeed, it was during the shooting of *Magic* on the Fox lot in Los Angeles that Joe bought back all the rights in *Gandhi* from Avco Embassy. He paid $100,000.

Tony Hopkins, who had scored such a success in *Bridge*, played Corky, the ventriloquist. His girlfriend, in a stunning performance, was portrayed by Ann-Margret, and his manager by the brilliant veteran American actor, Burgess Meredith. Ann-Margret's husband was played most effectively by Ed Lauter.

We began shooting on 30 January and finished on 29 March 1978. Tony, and indeed Ann-Margret, should have received international awards for their performances. They didn't, partly I think because of unjustified comparisons with the Ealing film of many years before, *Dead of Night*, on which so many of the critics suggested that Bill Goldman's script had been based. If they had taken the trouble to see the two films together, they would have realised their assumption was ludicrous. In addition to his study and understanding of the techniques of ventriloquism, Tony in particular gave a performance which I believe few actors could have equalled.

On completion of the shooting of *Magic*, Joe was prepared to

talk about *Gandhi* again. He now owned the rights, and he wanted Tony to play the lead. Tony, too, was fascinated at the prospect, and read a great deal of research material.

On my return to London to complete the editing and the dubbing of *Magic*, I learned the shocking news that Bob Bolt had been taken very seriously ill while working on a project with David Lean in Tahiti. I immediately got in touch with Peggy Ramsay, Bob's agent, who told me that there was no possibility of his writing for some considerable time. I still felt there was an enormous amount to do even on Bob's final screenplay and I would undoubtedly have asked him to work again on the script had he been able. However, with Joe's reassurances, I felt it was now or never, and I had no alternative but to press ahead. I believed I had acquired sufficient experience, both in terms of managing major productions and directing a considerable number of actors and actresses of varying skills and personalities, to undertake the production.

It was therefore essential, facing the cold truth of Bob's un-availability, to find another writer, and my mind went back to *Pope Joan* and Jack Briley.

8 Jack and I met in July 1978, and I outlined the background history of the Gandhi project, especially in regard to Bob Bolt. I asked him if he would care to work on Bob's script, and he said that before deciding he would naturally like to read it, then do some weeks of research. In the meantime, I talked to his agent, Douglas Rae, and we arrived at an agreement in principle.

On completing his period of gestation, Jack and I met again. He felt that the only way in which he could work on the subject would be to write his own original screenplay. After some thought I agreed, and by mid-October we had jointly worked out the broad outlines which would determine the script's shape. Joe was willing to finance Jack's screenplay, provided I participated in the payment. This I accepted—particularly in the knowledge that I had the chance of playing in Otto Preminger's film of Graham Greene's novel, *The Human Factor*.

In the middle of November I learned that Indiraji was staying at Claridges and, not having seen her for some time, I rang to ask if I might call on her. She looked very tired. There was no question that her defeat at the hands of Morarji Desai, following the election she called at the end of the Emergency, had taken its toll. Nevertheless, she was as warm in her greeting as ever, and I had some twenty minutes or so alone with her. We talked of the current situation in India, but inevitably the conversation turned to the film. She had no idea, under present circumstances, whether she would be able to be of any assistance, but was as keen as ever that the project should go forward.

Joe was impatient to see Jack's first attempt at the screenplay. However, he was also anxious for me to read the script of a television film which had been an enormous success in the States called *Verna – USO Girl*, based on a story by Paul Gallico. Joe now wanted to turn it into a major movie, and so, concurrently with the writing of Jack's screenplay, I gave a lot of thought to *Verna*.

In June, terms were agreed with Otto Preminger for me to play the part of Colonel Daintry in *The Human Factor*. However, before shooting started, Joe and I were very anxious to discover just what Tony Hopkins's attitude was towards *Gandhi*. His success in *Magic* meant he was now a name capable of attracting finance for a movie. He was playing Prospero in *The Tempest* in Los Angeles, and so I made one of those lunatic journeys, flying across the world one day, spending twenty-four hours with Tony and his wife, Jenni, and coming back the following morning. Without doubt, at that time he wanted to play Gandhi, which was a considerable encouragement both to Joe and to me.

Filming on *The Human Factor* finished in the middle of July. Otto had raised the finance from a series of independent sources, and anyone who is familiar with the problems surrounding such an operation has sympathy for the person concerned. Towards the end of shooting, he ran out of money and, as a result, a number of the actors, who were not as securely covered as the technicians, failed to receive their full salary. To the best of my knowledge that is still the situation, and the matter is in the hands of Equity, the actors' trade union.

Conference with Ben on the banks of the River Ganges.

Having committed a considerable proportion of what I expected to earn to Jack, I was placed in a very unfortunate position. I believe that had Otto, at the appropriate time, told us of his difficulties, everyone would have sympathised. However, he decided otherwise, and the result is that I certainly, and I believe others as well, feel somewhat cheated—in fact, even now I have only received just over fifty per cent of the monies due to me.

Rani Dube had always maintained a keen interest in *Gandhi*, and had constantly offered to give any assistance she could. With Indiraji out of office, my principal contact with government had disappeared and so, in contemplating my next trip to India in order to update our budget, and also to visit the new Prime Minister, Morarji Desai, I asked her to come with me. An appointment was arranged with Mr Desai, at which he endorsed the approval given by previous administrations. He reiterated, however, that before any final co-operation was offered, the Government would have to see the script. Naturally, we undertook to submit it on completion. From this visit it became apparent that our existing budget was woefully inadequate, and back in London we held meetings with Mike Stanley-Evans, who was to be Executive Producer, and our various accountants. The result was that we had to increase the last figure submitted to Joe by some fifty per cent.

On Bank Holiday Monday, August 27, an event occurred which horrified the entire world. Whilst on holiday at Mullaghmore, County Sligo, in Northern Ireland, Lord Louis, together with the Dowager Lady Brabourne, his grandson Nicholas, and a seventeen-year-old boatman, were murdered. A

As Independence is proclaimed, Gandhi spins in solitude at the ashram. *His own flagstaff is bare as he mourns the partition of the sub-Continent.*

bomb hidden by the IRA blew the boat in which they were sailing to smithereens. His daughter and son-in-law, Lord and Lady Brabourne, and their son Timothy were most severely injured, and for some days their lives too hung in the balance. To their eternal shame, the terrorists, whoever they were, by their barbaric and mindless action killed not only one of the most brilliant and well loved men of his time but also probably the most liberal member of the royal family that we have been fortunate enough to know. I so often recall his many kindnesses to me, and I shall be ever in his debt, as evidenced, I hope, by the fact that *Gandhi* is dedicated—together with Motilal Kothari and Pandit Nehru—to his memory.

Sardar Patel is played by Saeed Jaffrey.

I postponed my planned trip to New York in order that Sheila and I might attend Lord Louis' funeral at Westminster Abbey. John and Patricia Brabourne have been friends of mine for many years, and during all the ups and downs on the Gandhi film, John's advice and encouragement have always been of tremendous comfort. It therefore meant a great deal to me that when they eventually saw *Gandhi* they not only thought well of it, but wrote me a most touching letter.

Following my visit to New York, during which Joe accepted the revised budget, I read Jack's first draft. Even at that stage, it seemed to me much the most successful of the scripts so far written. Jack is not easy to work with. When he has an idea fixed in his mind it is almost impossible to budge him. There were, however, several key sequences he had omitted, which I felt had to be included. Throughout the latter part of September and the whole of October, we met daily to discuss the revisions. The next draft was completed by early November, and was sent by courier to New York. Joe read it at once, and rang me in some excitement, pronouncing apart from anything else that it was the first 'commercial' script he had read on the subject.

He was also now in receipt of the budget that we had prepared for *Verna*. It seemed prohibitively high, and he disputed it hotly. I believe he thought I was so prejudiced in favour of *Gandhi* that I had minimised its cost, whilst exaggerating that of *Verna*. This, of course, was not true. Apart from being dishonest, it would have been a very stupid action, and one which in the end result would not have fooled Joe for one moment. He believed that the Gandhi project still required some additional box office ingredient, which, as yet, we did not have. Joe also wished me to discuss with British television the possibilities of their purchasing *Gandhi*,

and I went to see Alasdair Milne, at that time Managing Director of Television at the BBC, and then Gunnar Rugheimer, who was in charge of programme acquisition. Both were interested, and we eventually concluded a very good deal. However, at the back of my mind, partly because of his fascination with *Verna*, was the nagging doubt as to whether Joe really would go forward with the production, despite his enthusiasm for the script.

Therefore, since my American agent, Marti Baum, said he had a number of other offers for me, I went to Los Angeles. Marti, together with his partner, Mike Ovitz, the founder of Creative Artists Agency, endorsed my scepticism. However, I would not be shaken in my belief that *Gandhi* had a future. Marti and Mike lost patience with me and said that perpetually turning down offer after offer was tantamount to wrecking my directorial career. In addition to a firm proposal to direct James Clavell's *Taipan*, they also had a series of similar propositions for me, including Stanley Jaffe's film *Father Sky*, a terrific script which was eventually shown under the title *Taps*.

Before leaving for the States, Joe had suggested that I should sound out possible deals with both Rank and EMI. On my return I learned that they had both declined. Barry Spikings of EMI said he liked the script very much, but his associates felt the subject matter was uncommercial. Tony Williams, Rank's head of production, was tremendously enthusiastic, and had recommended it to his board. However, their decision was also negative.

By the turn of the year I was beginning to wonder whether

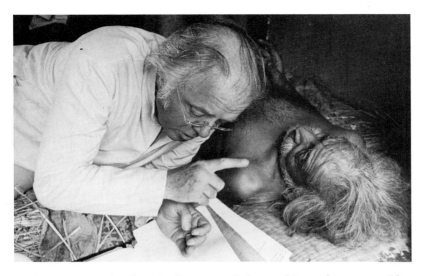

Marti Baum and Mike Ovitz were right, and I ought to consider seriously some of the offers that were still on the table. I felt I needed some particular spur to regain Joe's enthusiasm and it materialised in the person of Jackie Baroda.

Out of the blue, he telephoned to say that he was in London, and to inquire whether there was any news of the film, since if he could still be of any assistance he would be delighted. I went to see him. Together with all of us who are devoted to Mrs Gandhi, he was thrilled by the extent of her victory in the elections in the first week of January 1980, and consequently in high spirits. I received a letter from him dated 6 February in which he guaranteed to put up fifty per cent of the finance for the film. It was just what I needed, and I rang Joe.

Having made his own inquiries, and on discovering that the Maharaja of Baroda was a force to be reckoned with, he rang me to say that we should go ahead. The three of us eventually met in London at Joe's suite in the Dorchester on 6 March. Joe was so certain that he wanted to proceed that he brought his lawyer with him from New York. Jackie signed a contract, agreeing that either he or a colleague of his would lodge letters of credit with a major London bank up to a total of $10 million worth of rupees. This Joe was certain would enable him to raise the rest of the money quite easily. There was an atmosphere of euphoria. Joe and Jackie, not dissimilar in stature, or for that matter in their enthusiasm, vowed that together we would make one of the great movies of all time. Joe returned to New York that same night.

ON FOLLOWING PAGE
With the creation of Hindu India and Muslim Pakistan, millions of refugees flee from one new State to the other.

We used a helicopter to film the refugee columns, which stretched for several miles.

The following day I had meetings with Jackie and his legal advisers, who, one has to say, were not happy with the form of the agreement Jackie had signed, since it involved certain personal guarantees which they felt he might not be able to fulfil. Jackie returned to India, and I continued to negotiate with his lawyers. They expressed the view that, although His Highness's intention to participate in setting up the film was evident, there were nevertheless a number of financial details which had to be arranged prior to his signing a more formal contract.

In the circumstances, I had to point out very forcibly that it was Jackie Baroda who had volunteered to back the film in this way, and that the initiative had been entirely his and not mine. I managed to speak to Jackie on the phone in Delhi, and he was reassuring about his ability to fulfil his undertakings, and in particular to arrange for the pre-production funds. He asked me again to talk to his solicitors, but most important of all to come to Delhi as soon as possible in order to discuss the project with him personally, and of course to see Mrs Gandhi.

I made a number of attempts to reach his lawyer. He by now appeared to be avoiding my calls, and I therefore sent a letter by hand. Obviously matters were not as they should be. The guarantees for pre-production which had been promised had not materialised, and despite further efforts to speak to Jackie by phone, I never managed to do so. I subsequently learned that he had gone to Lahore with the Indian cricket team and was, to all intents and purposes, incommunicado. I cancelled the trip that I had planned for India, and again attempted to reach his solicitors, but without success. Joe, ironically, in the meantime, announced that he was confident of being able to find all the rest of the money required from American cable and network sources, if the rupees were made available. At the conclusion of our successful meetings in March, I had suggested that we should celebrate Jackie's fiftieth birthday at our home in Richmond, announcing our tripartite commitment to make the picture. Joe, however, was becoming more and more sceptical about Jackie's involvement, admittedly not without grounds, and now flatly declined to come to London for the birthday party. He further announced that the whole occasion was, in his opinion, a grave error.

Jackie landed in London on 30 March, and we had several meetings with his errant lawyers. Although some of the negotiations were inevitably delicate, a situation was arrived at whereby once again there were assurances that the pre-production funds would be forthcoming. The party was on Wednesday, 2 April. Jackie arrived looking every inch a maharaja, and announced to the assembled company at the end of the evening that he would be backing the production of *Gandhi*.

Over the Easter weekend I had as unpleasant a transatlantic phone conversation as I can recall. Joe had some pretty tough things to say about Jackie, but his principal invective was reserved for the Indian Government's recognition of the Palestine Liberation Organisation. As far as he was concerned, he said, 'That was that'. He certainly didn't intend to proceed with the film. 'You won't find a dollar to back it. Nobody is interested in backing a film on Gandhi—certainly if you haven't got any rupees, and you obviously haven't. You'd better have it, Dickie. I'll let you have it.' As soon as the office opened after the bank holiday, I wrote Joe a long letter, which read in part:

> 'While there is a hope, Joe, of the picture being made, I know that I must hang on and pursue every avenue. I have over nearly twenty years given up an enormous amount in order to make this film in which I believe so passionately. Indeed, over the past few years I have turned down a quite extraordinary number of other opportunities. I feel, how-ever, that this subject is more important to me than anything else in my professional life and I am, therefore, prepared to stick by it until production this year becomes utterly

Rohini Hattangady washes clothes for over an hour, awaiting the right formation of birds to cross the sky.

Inevitably the bitterness of the refugees creates clashes and these escalate into an inter-religious bloodbath, so widespread that the authorities cannot begin to control it.

impossible. I fully understand your reluctance to become further committed under the present circumstances, and I suppose I have to admit, however reluctantly, that perhaps in the light of your current feelings I ought to see if it is possible to accept your suggestion to "let me have it". I was somewhat bowled over when you said on the phone, "You'd better have it, Dickie. I'll let you have it." We've worked together on this for many, many years and it seems inconceivable that we should not see it go into production together, but if you feel this strongly I have no alternative but to accept your decision.

'Obviously I am not in a position personally to be able to put cash on the table as of this moment. Nevertheless, were I able to mount the production, one could certainly include in the initial budget the financing of the sum which you would require in terms of my repurchasing the rights. There would then follow of course whatever further sums and/or percentage you thought appropriate. Perhaps if your present feelings remain, you would consider what sort of proposal you would like to suggest.

'As soon as I have any further definite information, I will call you. I still believe, Joe, that together we could make one of the most important films that has ever been produced, and I pray you will reconsider your opinion. If not, however, I really must attempt—even if such an attempt is ultimately abortive—to go it alone. Yours ever, Dickie.'

The following day I received a telex signed by William Goldberg as Vice President of Joseph E. Levine Presents, in which I was told that under no circumstances had I the authority to make any commitments in regard to the property which their company owned.

On receipt of this, I rang Joe in New York, explaining I'd written a long letter, crossing with their telex, which he would be receiving shortly. Joe restated his complete lack of faith in Jackie Baroda, and said categorically, 'I think we ought to have a severance. I'll let you have it. You have it.' I replied, 'All right, Joe, I accept.'

A few days later, on Tuesday, 15 April, I was informed by a representative of Jackie Baroda that a letter had been received, authorising a '*loan*, to the value of $900,000 on an overdraft basis, judged daily at two per cent over base rate, all amounts

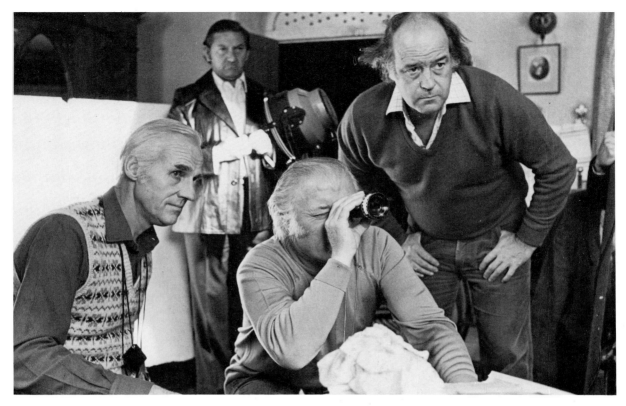

outstanding to be repaid by 14 July'. Obviously this was quite unacceptable, and did not comply in any way with the arrangements, both written and verbal, that we had previously agreed upon.

Nevertheless, Baroda or no Baroda, Jack Briley's script, in which I had invested not only hard cash but also hours and hours of time, persuaded me to keep going. It was by now a really successful amalgam of all the ingredients I felt were vital, whilst at the same time being a sufficiently moving and dramatic story to become a successful three-hour movie.

Several days before these new developments I had given the script to a mutual friend of Joe's and mine, Ascania Branca, the Managing Director of Twentieth Century-Fox in the UK. Both Joe and I had previously mentioned the subject to him, and now he expressed an unreserved enthusiasm for its potential and said he would like to discuss it with Fox in Los Angeles.

Due to the uncertainty of the Baroda situation, Rani Dube and I had several meetings to discuss our next move. She had

Lining up a shot with Billy Williams (left), whose camera work has contributed such an enormous amount to the film, with Chic Anstiss (right), the Camera Operator, and with Sound Recordist, Simon Kaye, looking on.

joined the company as Co-Producer and it was agreed that she should proceed to India, in the knowledge that Jackie's investment was questionable, to see if she could confirm any of the alternative forms of backing which had been discussed with a number of people. I followed her on 16 April, certain that the prerequisite to any further progress must be the approval of Jack's script.

The day after my arrival, Indiraji invited me for dinner. It was very informal. Sanjay, Rajiv, their wives and children were present. After the usual pleasantries, the topic was inevitably the film, and I soon gained the impression that the Prime Minister was herself beginning to share some of my frustration in our inability to start the production, with which she, too, had been associated for some seventeen years. I explained that, in addition to all the other problems, the real concern at present was that of the finance. In my opinion, our ability to raise non-rupee funds from one source or another was unquestionable and if only I could count on the Indian funding I really did believe the picture could go into production at the end of the current year.

'What is the problem with the rupee finance?' she inquired.

I explained that a number of people, some directly, some through intermediaries, had indicated they wished to invest, but despite all our efforts, nothing had actually been confirmed.

She suggested that a copy of the script should formally be submitted to the Ministry of Information and Broadcasting, and that she would have a word with Vasant Sathe, the minister concerned, to see if there was any way in which the Government, possibly through the National Film Development Corporation, could ensure the necessary rupees. She was not giving any guarantees whatsoever, since this might ultimately involve a Cabinet decision, but nevertheless she would suggest that the Ministry might look into the matter.

The family all went to bed, and Indiraji and I continued to talk for another half hour or so before I took my leave. Tucking the script under her arm, she bade me good-night with the words, 'Well, this will provide me with a little bed-time reading.'

Rani now really came into her own. Within a matter of days we were meeting every official who might be necessary to the furtherance of the project. She seemed to know them all. In addition, she introduced me to her friend Mr Radhakrishna, who was the Secretary of the Gandhi Peace Foundation. A large man with a beatific smile, he impressed me enormously, not only by

178

Rani Dube and I were fortunate enough to be permitted a brief meeting with Acharya Kripalani in hospital during the last few weeks of his life.

his gentle but determined interest in the film, but also by his overt willingness to help us forward our plans.

While in Bombay she took me to meet a great friend of hers, Dolly Thakore, who is both an actress and a television news announcer. Rani suggested she should act as our Casting Director and possibly assist with the Indian press. I also went to see Gandhi's biographer, B. R. Nanda. I had, of course, met him previously at the suggestion of Pandit Nehru, but on this occasion I was able to give him Jack's script, asking if we might meet again to hear his comments.

All these events took place concurrently with our meetings at the Ministry of Information and Broadcasting. They were led by the Minister, Mr Sathe, whilst the detailed discussions were under the care of Mr A. K. Dutt, the Secretary to the Ministry. He has in fact now moved to another post, but unmistakably his kind assistance aided our ability to plough our way through all the inevitable bureaucracy.

Vasant Sathe, the Minister who defended the Government's involvement in *Gandhi* both privately and publicly, is a man with his own particular charisma. He is very tall, with pitch black hair and eyes which seem permanently half-closed as a result of the grin which frequently flits across his face, disappearing only when his eyes almost pop out of his head as he professes total surprise or bewilderment at some development in the conversation. His civil servants, inevitably, were motivated by an innate caution in committing themselves too hastily, but he was prepared, with Mr Dutt, to forge ahead with all necessary speed.

A day or so before I left, I saw Indiraji again. She had read the script on two successive nights, between 1.30 and 3.00 a.m. She thought it remarkably successful in containing so succinctly the vital elements necessary to tell such a story. She had one or two pertinent criticisms, particularly with regard to the early relationship between Gandhi and Kasturba. She thought that the film should have a foreword, explaining the omission of many incidents and personalities which would be missed by those familiar with this epoch in India's history. She also felt that we should admit to straying from strict fact in terms of date and time, since it would be impossible to grant every moment its allotted space in a film lasting three hours. She said, however, that the Government should not *approve* the script, since the film must be the creation of its makers. Government and the Ministry should merely satisfy themselves that, related to the subject matter, the manner in which the film was envisaged was a proper one.

I thanked her for finding the time in her incredibly busy life to read the screenplay and said that I would be leaving the next day, following the last formal meeting with the Minister. I had earlier been asked to send a letter to the National Film Development Corporation, inviting their association as investors in the production. That day I had received their agreement in principle with the suggestion that the machinery should be set up for working out the details. Finally, on the afternoon of our departure, in the presence of the Minister, I was handed a letter signed by the Joint Secretary for the Ministry, which assured me of the Government's full co-operation in facilitating the production, including 'arrangements for ensuring the rupee portion of the investment required for the project'.

Rani and I had achieved an enormous amount in under three weeks, and we returned to London feeling well satisfied. I rang Joe and suggested that I should come to New York to discuss the developments in India and to learn his up-to-date views.

I arrived in New York by Concorde on the morning of 19 May and went straight to his office. His greeting was polite, but could scarcely be described as abounding with *bonhomie*. He repeated that I had made a grave tactical error in proceeding with Baroda's birthday party and, bearing in mind that Baroda had reneged on his agreement as far as Joe was concerned, considered the occasion a personal insult. He said that he had learned from someone who was present at the party that we had never mentioned his name in any of the toasts, which was a further insult. He then added that, through a great friend who made films in India, he had heard that I was peddling his subject to every third-class Indian distributor. Since both pieces of hearsay were untrue I denied them emphatically, and told Joe that the only discussions that I had had were with the NFDC at the request of the Prime Minister.

He insisted on reminding me that I had no right to mention his name, because I hadn't as yet paid him for the subject. I told him that I had in no way used his name in India, then I pointed out that a great deal of the script was mine, since I was largely responsible for its original concept and shape, and furthermore, without approval from the Indian Government, it was absolutely worthless. Therefore, whether he owned it or I owned it, or we owned it jointly was immaterial and anything I had done in terms of gaining government approval could only enhance the value of the script.

He told me that I was to go and see Bill Goldberg who would inform me of the terms on which I could repurchase the property.

The first condition was that I would have a sixty-day option,

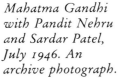

Mahatma Gandhi with Pandit Nehru and Sardar Patel, July 1946. An archive photograph.

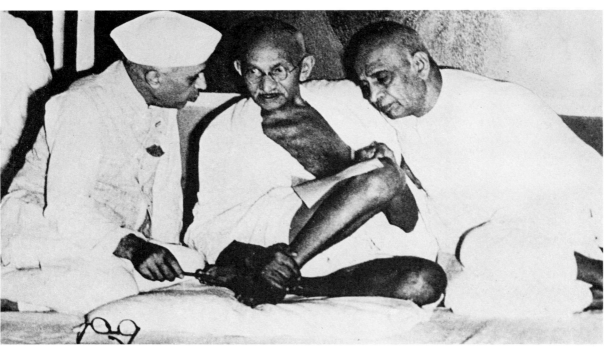

Before his last fast and accompanied by Abdul Gaffar Khan, Gandhi visits a village in Bihar ravaged by the Hindu/Muslim disturbances. An archive photograph.

for which I would have to pay a quarter of a million dollars. I needn't put up cash—Joe already held over $150,000 of my percentage from *Bridge* and *Magic*—and he was prepared to take the entire sum from the profits that would be ultimately due to me. During the sixty-day period, if I wished to purchase the rights, I had to commit to the payment of a further three-quarters of a million dollars on the first day of shooting, and another million dollars on the last day of shooting—a total of two million dollars—plus 7.5 per cent of the net profits, or 2.5 per cent of the gross profits, whichever was the greater.

I asked Bill Goldberg what would happen if, at the end of the option period, I had not set up the film. He replied that I would lose all the rights, together with any further benefits which might accrue to them, and that they would revert to Mr Levine.

Never, in all honesty, have I been quite so shattered. I went back into Joe's office. Without any preamble he said, 'Do you accept?' I replied that I thought the terms were unbelievable. 'Well, I want to know,' he said. 'Do you accept, or not?'

I said I considered the sixty-day option period was totally impractical and he agreed to consult his lawyer and speak to me later. It was finally conceded that the option would be for nine months.

I rang Marti Baum in Los Angeles and told him the terms. He said that under no circumstances must I accept them—if I did he would never speak to me again. I told him that no matter how unpalatable they were, I proposed to agree, since I still wished to make the film more than anything in my entire professional career. His reply was that I had to be insane.

The next day I signed the prepared document. I left Joe's office, and I remember going down in the lift utterly devastated and close to tears. It was a dreadful end to what in many ways had been a profound friendship. Having gone through so many years with him, having made two films together, always with the hope of making *Gandhi* as a team, I found the manner of our parting hugely distressing. Apart from a very brief phone call, I have not spoken to him since. The result of the deal was that there was no way in which I could draw any form of salary if the film was ever set up. The terms he demanded were so onerous that whatever my remuneration might be I felt certain it would have to be deferred until the entire cost of the film had been recouped. This in fact proved to be the case.

Rani was convinced that our time in India had been successful, and her faith was justified when I received two official telegrams from Mr Dutt, saying that 'funds would be released for the proposed film venture', despite the necessity for unavoidable procedural routines. 'In the meantime, however,' the second telegram concluded, 'we request you go ahead with your plans.'

Following a meeting with Ascania Branca and Tim Hampton,

Finishing touches as we prepare to shoot a scene with South African actor/playwright, Athol Fugard, who plays General Smuts.

Head of European Production, I decided to go to Los Angeles to see Fox. However, a couple of days before I left Jack Briley came over to see me. He had been working with a new transatlantic partnership, International Film Investors of New York presided over by Josiah Child, and in London Goldcrest Film International, under the control of John D. Eberts. They admired Jack considerably, and he suggested that as a fallback in case the Fox deal did not go through I should go and see Mr Eberts.

I went to their offices in Chesterfield Street to meet Jake, as he's known. He's in his late thirties, a very tall, bespectacled curly-headed Canadian, with the most engaging stutter, one which I'm certain he uses to the greatest possible effect when he believes it appropriate. He undertook to read the script that very night. He was bowled over by it, and convinced that he and his partner ought to participate in the production. As a result, it was agreed that I should go to Los Angeles via New York in order to see Jo Child. If the deal went through with Fox, and there was any room for IFI/GFI to be involved, then this they would like. If, on the other hand, the Fox deal failed Jake's view was that they would wish to put up the risk money to start the production going, with the hope of raising the remaining funds for shooting in the Fall.

From the airport, just before boarding Concorde, I made one last desperate attempt to contact Barry Spikings, who had been promising to reconsider his decision in regard to EMI's participation even for a nominal sum since I was anxious that the picture should have some British connection. He came out of a meeting and told me the reply was no. I said, 'Is there nothing EMI would wish to contribute even in terms of a nominal figure?' No—those in charge of distribution felt *Gandhi* had no commercial potential at all. 'Didn't they like the script?' Incredibly, the answer was they had not even read it.

On reaching New York. I went to see Jo Child, who had now read the script. He confirmed Jake's proposals, and went so far as to say he would guarantee a million dollars there and then towards pre-production as pure risk money, so highly did he regard the film's potential.

I next rang Marti Baum in Los Angeles. He told me that the Fox people would all be back from Europe within a day or so. In the meantime, I was to meet David Field, right-hand man to Sherry Lansing, the newly appointed President of Production. David, as engaging a chap as one could wish to meet, read the

With Ian Charleson, who plays Charlie Andrews.

Crowds gather at the house in Calcutta where Gandhi has undertaken to fast unto death unless all violence ceases.

script and was so enthusiastic that he came over to my hotel early the following morning. He rang Sherry Lansing and told her, in my hearing, that he thought Fox must do *Gandhi*. A few days later I met Sherry, Norman Levy, David Field, Emil Buisse, Jean Louis Roubin and Peter Meyer in Los Angeles, together of course with Marti Baum. The tone of the discussions, with some slight reservation, seemed immensely optimistic. Certainly Norman Levy believed that Fox should make a major investment in the film and said as much forcibly at the meeting. Marti and I left the studios convinced we would be receiving a very exciting offer.

Almost inexplicably, however, the proposal was turned down. Sherry Lansing, having consulted her colleagues, was of the opinion that *Gandhi* was uncommercial, and therefore, despite the enthusiasm voiced by Norman Levy and David Field in particular, she said no. Subsequently a revised proposition was put forward, which Marti, Jo and I decided to decline on the supposition that IFI and GFI would put together the entire non-Indian financing.

The fact that *Gandhi* ever went into production was due initially to Jo Child and Jake Eberts. Jo's participation was limited to approximately one million dollars. The vast majority of the rest of the backing was acquired, in one form or another, by Jake on behalf of GFI. Their principal shareholder is Pearson Longman, whose Chief Executive, James Lee, was as enthusiastic as Jake, and in the final analysis it is these two men who are responsible for the film being made.

The whole setting-up period must have been a nightmare for Jake. Time after time finance which appeared to be secure disappeared. Legal complications were endless, and his various trips to India to meet not only the ministries involved but also the NFDC, were gruelling occasions. The newly appointed Managing Director of NFDC, Malati Tambey Vaidya, was in a particularly difficult position in having to deal with what was a commercial enterprise through the auspices of a government-sponsored organisation. However, with the backing of the new Joint Secretary to the Minister of Information and Broadcasting, Suresh Mathur, who was a tower of strength, the project moved inexorably forward.

In my imagination I had always envisaged a particular day upon which the film would be formally announced as going into production. It never happened. On my return from Los Angeles, we were already under way. Mike was planning our complex shooting schedule, and Terry Clegg had taken charge of production. One of the best decisions I made was to engage Stuart Craig, the Art Director on *A Bridge Too Far*, as Production Designer. He is a relatively young man, and *Gandhi* was the largest movie he had undertaken. Not only did he prove to be highly efficient, which was essential, since the Art Department falling behind schedule could bring the whole production to a halt, but he also proved massively creative.

With Geoff Unsworth no longer alive, my second vital decision was who to select as Cameraman. Mike and I finally decided to approach Billy Williams, whose work on *Eagle's Wing* and *On Golden Pond* had recently gained him such enormous credit. He collected the script and undertook to let me know his

187

answer the following morning. I received a telegram. It read, 'Dear Dickie. Yes. Love Billy.'

Michael (Chalkie) White had been working with me ever since he acted as my Assistant on *Magic*, and was, with Lorna Mueller, our Researcher, now crammed with knowledge about Gandhiji. The offices became a hive of activity augmented by our assistant accountant Terry Mellis.

At the end of June, having been preceded by Stuart Craig and his Supervising Art Director, Bob Laing, who now had a series of particular locations to show us, Mike and I, together with a full recce crew, left once again for India.

Rani and I had a mass of meetings with various ministries and, although obtaining the necessary approvals was frustratingly time-consuming, somehow Rani always managed to cut through the bureaucratic undergrowth. During this period, one task that obsessed me almost more than any other was the casting of the principal characters but, overriding all, that of Gandhi himself. I had combed India for possibilities, but without success. By now, Tony Hopkins had finally decided that for him the problems of playing an Indian were insuperable. During the negotiations with Fox, everybody had talked enthusiastically of John Hurt. I knew him of course from *Ten Rillington Place*, and he had just scored two great successes in *Midnight Express* and *The Elephant Man*. After a number of discussions it was agreed that we would test him, not to see if he was capable of playing the part—that went without saying—but to discover whether he might prove acceptable as an Indian.

Concurrently I also had in mind an actor whom I had always felt was a strong possibility. His name was Ben Kingsley, one of the leading players in the Royal Shakespeare Company. I had seen him first many years beforehand in Peter Brook's *A Midsummer Night's Dream*, and in a number of productions since, culminating in Bertolt Brecht's *Baal*. His principal advocate was my son, Michael, who judged him as superb an actor as any working in England. Talent apart, Ben had the considerable advantage of having an Indian father, obviously heightening his acceptability as Gandhiji and I was always determined that he should be amongst those we tested.

However, during our visit to India the most important question was the casting of Gandhiji's wife, Kasturba. Dolly Thakore arranged for me to see innumerable Indian actresses on stage, in an endless succession of Hindi films and in person. I was

Candice Bergen promised to play the part of Margaret Bourke-White fifteen years before we started shooting.

Rehearsing with Geraldine James.

very taken by a young actress called Smita Patil, who seemed to have real talent, and cinematically her personality worked remarkably well. She was, however, very beautiful, perhaps too beautiful. I also saw the distinguished actress, Bhakti Barwe, playing in the theatre, and asked her if she was prepared to come to London to take a screen test. I nevertheless felt I still had not found the ideal Kasturba.

Then Dolly rang me one afternoon, asking if I could delay my return to London by a day or so, since she had found several other artists she wanted me to see. I remember her bringing five of them to my hotel room near Bombay airport. One was a girl named Rohini Hattangady. As she came through the door, I think my heart missed a beat. She seemed instantly to have the essential qualities that I sought for the personality of Kasturba.

Her mother-tongue was Marathi, and that night I saw her in the theatre. She appeared as two different characters, firstly as a young, feline, sensual seductress and secondly a character in such contrast that for the first minute or two I simply did not recognise her—a senile, eighty-year-old matriarch. Her talent was undoubted. The question was whether she could be sufficiently fluent in English and whether her talent would transfer—which is not always the case—to film. She too, with Bhakti and Smita, agreed to come to London.

I had always wanted Saeed Jaffrey, with whom I'd appeared in *The Chess Players*, to accept the part of Sardar Patel, and fortunately he agreed.

189

Leaving the Art Department to continue working in India, the rest of us returned to London and the screen tests took place at Shepperton Studios during the last week of July. The three Indian actresses had worked extremely hard on the dialogue and, together with Johnnie Hurt and Ben Kingsley, their shooting was completed over a period of three days.

I decided that we should view Johnnie Hurt's test with him alone. Before it had been on the screen for thirty seconds it was evident to him and to the rest of us that a European attempting to play an Indian would be utterly unconvincing. Professional that he is, he removed all embarrassment from the occasion by describing his legs as those of a second-row rugby forward, rather than an ascetic from the Indian sub-continent.

As far as the girls were concerned, the decision lay between Rohini and Smita. Smita's test was eminently professional, and

Having learnt of Gandhi's fast on the terrace of a Muslim house in riot-torn Calcutta, Prime Minister Nehru arrives from Delhi.

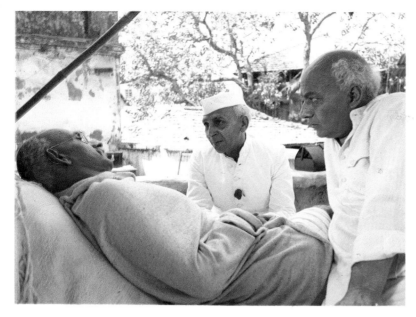

Nehru and his Deputy Prime Minister, Sardar Patel, beg Gandhi to end his fast.

very moving. Rohini's was equally fine, but in her case there was a remarkable affinity to the particular character of Kasturba—a Gujarati provincial girl living at the turn of the century. With skilful make-up I also believed she could achieve the age-span from twenties to early seventies.

Finally, there was Ben Kingsley. He was a miracle. He burst out of the screen with a credibility and with a magnetism that one could scarcely have contemplated. His eyes were mesmeric, and his physical frame—provide he lost some weight—was right. He even wore his *dhoti* as though it was part of his everyday garb. It appeared to all of us that if there was one actor on earth who could play the part of Gandhiji with conviction, it was Ben.

I was thrilled, since I had always felt that ideally Gandhiji should be played by an actor who was unfamiliar to cinema audiences, and this, to all intents and purposes, would be Ben's first film. Unlike so many others over the years, our backers Jake and Jo agreed with this philosophy, and rejoiced in the discovery of such a unique talent.

It was now vital that I started to assemble the shooting crew. Fortunately Simon Kaye, the best Sound Recordist in the UK, could join me again. Johnnie Bloom, who had cut *Magic* so brilliantly, was working with Karel Reisz on *The French Lieutenant's Woman*, but he was greatly anxious to edit *Gandhi* and so I agreed that he should join us half-way through the shooting period and that Chris Ridsdale should take charge of the cutting meanwhile.

I was also keen to persuade David Tomblin to become First Assistant Director. His talents are very special. I do not know of any other 'First' who could have coped as he had with a production on the scale of *A Bridge Too Far* and who, considering the additional problems of logistics and communications in India, would be so well equipped to deal with *Gandhi*. Without David and his two lieutenants, Steve Lanning and Roy Button, we would never have been able to complete the film within our stringent schedule. It was through David that I met June Randall who had been working with him as Continuity on *Raiders of the Lost Ark*, and her equanimity and energy in India proved both infectious and inexhaustible.

More importantly almost than anyone, I wanted Tom Smith to be in charge of make-up. He adds a touch of genius. He made me up for *The Dock Brief*, and I believed that his wizardry in ageing artists imperceptibly was vital to our principal characters' credibility. Slowly, being spurred on by the unique collection of reference pictures with which we challenged him, Tom was finally seduced into going abroad for so long. We also managed to recruit as Chief Hairdresser Paula Gillespie, whose outstanding craftsmanship complemented Tom's work perfectly.

I asked Diana Hawkins, who had been my Personal Assistant for five years, to return to her true profession and become Director of Publicity for the production. Years before, she had been in charge of publicity for Allied Film Makers, and was then the youngest and certainly one of the very finest publicists in the British film industry before leaving to become a novelist. Diana's acceptance meant I needed a new PA and I was fortunate enough to find Clare Howard, who joined me on 13 October, a few weeks before we were all to leave for India. She has been a tower of strength and on occasions I really would not have got through without her.

Before shooting started, every few days I would have a session with Jack Briley. He was always open to debate, although it was evident that every syllable in his screenplay had been weighed minutely. Both of us had various minor amendments to put forward, but there were in my opinion one or two sequences which were simply beyond our financial and schedule capabilities. Fighting over every word, Jack ultimately agreed to cut them. In July 1980 ten copies of the script were dispatched via the diplomatic bag to New Delhi.

Together with Jack, Terry Clegg, Rani and Pat Howell, our

chief accountant, I left for India on 3 August. We were greeted at the airport by my friend of some twelve years standing, Mohini Banerji. Mo and her retired Air Vice-Marshal husband, Banjo, who was the film's military adviser, had been constant companions on all my trips. She had taken leave of absence from her job with an Indian charity in order to manage our production offices and was already established at the Ashok Hotel, where we were also to house the wardrobe and make-up departments and where the majority of the crew would stay during the pre-production period and the actual shooting in Delhi.

Suresh Jindal, the producer of *The Chess Players*, whom I had hoped might be able to join us was now, in fact, our Associate Producer in overall charge of the recruitment and management of the Indian side of the operation. He had been able to obtain as Production Manager the services of Shama Habibullah, who enjoyed a considerable reputation in the Indian film industry. It was a great joy to me that Vala Kothari took a key position on the crew and so continued the family involvement.

We were also fortunate enough to engage Bhanu Athaiya, India's leading costume designer, and the veracity of the period clothes worn both by the huge crowds and the principal actors is due not only to her eagle eye but also to that of Sina Kaul, who never left the set from dawn until late at night.

Two other stalwarts from *Bridge* joined us in Delhi; Loretta Ordewer as Production Assistant and Judith Bunn as Location Secretary. Although they worked six days a week from six in the morning to ten at night and put in considerable office hours on

Chalkie White prepared preliminary sketches with a transparent overlay to give an idea of how Ben Kingsley might look when made up as Gandhi.

Accompanied by his Muslim colleague, Azad, Nehru tells a crowd in Calcutta that unless all rioting ceases Gandhi will inevitably die.

what, for most of the other crew, was our one rest day, their efficiency and unfailing good humour never deserted them throughout the many months they spent in India. The same was true of Margaret Adams, linked to us by telex and in charge of all our London affairs from the office in Richmond.

In India we met the officials from the ministries primarily involved in the production, under the chairmanship of Suresh Mathur, together with the representatives from the National Film Development Corporation led by Anil Dharkar. Anil was, at that time, Administrative Officer to the Corporation, and evidently knowledgeable about film production in India. There was much discussion related to the various costs involved, together with the appropriate salaries that should be paid. The differentials between varying members of the crew, whether British or Indian, and questions of large-scale accommodation were thoroughly debated. The budget was dissected, analysed and ultimately accepted by both parties.

We all recognised that there was bound to be public controversy both in regard to government involvement in a production which was essentially commercial in concept, and over the principle of a foreigner making a film about the father of the Indian nation. Furthermore, there always had been debate as to whether the film should be made at all. However, the furore started with a quite extraordinary attack by one of the Lok Dal leaders, George Fernandes. At a press conference he announced that in his opinion the making of the film was 'a sell-out of the country's honour'. He then listed a series of observations about the film, all based on pure supposition. He criticised the financial set-up, of which he had no knowledge, and derided the script, which he had never seen. The sad thing was that this, in my judgement, set a tenor of criticism which surrounded the film in the ensuing months.

The group which did seem to me to have a case, deserving a thorough answer, was the Forum for Better Cinema. They complained it was inequitable that the Indian Government should be investing sums on such a scale in a film made by a predominantly foreign company when Indian film makers were starved of finance. This was a situation with which I had much sympathy, being an independent producer myself. It was for this reason that I extracted an unequivocal statement from the Ministry of Information and Broadcasting that any sums devoted to the Gandhi film would in no way erode the backing that was available for indigenous film production. In addition, I received an assurance from the Minister that if any profit accrued to the investment made by the NFDC it would be ploughed back into Indian production.

I also believed that if the Gandhi film proved to be successful in terms of logistics it would be a beneficial experience for Indian technicians in exactly the same way that those in the British film industry have benefited from American films made in the United Kingdom, and should result in an influx of further co-productions which would never previously have been considered viable. That belief has, I am glad to say, been borne out—at least six major foreign productions and co-productions have been set up in India since the completion of *Gandhi*.

It was gratifying that the Forum for Better Cinema condemned other views put forward that our film should not be undertaken by a foreigner. They observed, with I thought some justification, that it was over thirty years since the Mahatma's death, and no

We filmed John Gielgud's scenes as Lord Irwin in London.

Indian company had attempted to make such a film in all that time.

Finally, there were those who were opposed to the film being made under any circumstances. They believed that Gandhiji was 'a phenomenon and not a mere man' who could not possibly be portrayed by an actor, and that it was sacrilegious to attempt to depict such a form of deity in terms of commercial cinema. Not unnaturally, I totally disagreed with their view, continuing to use Pandit Nehru's words as my touchstone. It seemed to me infinitely important that the words and faith of this remarkable man should be known to the widest possible number of people. One dear lady actually announced that the only way in which Gandhiji could be portrayed would be by a moving light, and I'm afraid I was impertinent enough to riposte that I wasn't 'making a film about bloody Tinker Bell'.

We continued with our casting. Alyque Padamsee, the theatre director and actor, was to play Mohamed Ali Jinnah. The distinguished Shreeram Lagoo agreed to play Professor Gokhale and we also cast several boys from the National School of Drama, including Virendra Razdan as Maulana Azad, Anang Desai as Kripalani and Pankaj Kapoor as Pyarelal Nayar, Bapu's final secretary and biographer.

Although current rupee funding had been undertaken by the Ministry on a *pro tem* basis, final approval of the agreement between Indo-British Films and the NFDC required a formal Cabinet decision. I was anxious to get back to London to deal with the mass of details still needing attention. I was, however, certain that it would be folly to leave India without written notice of the Cabinet's approval in my possession.

196

Due to the many important issues higher on their agenda, they did not reach this particular item at the expected meeting. I therefore had to postpone my return by three days and well recall the suspense while Mo, Banjo, Rani and I waited in Room 542 at the Ashok Hotel for a phone call to say that all was well.

I received the letter by hand late that night, allowing me to catch the morning plane. It was signed by the redoubtable Mr Dutt as Secretary to the Ministry of Information and Broadcasting, and contained the phrases that I so longed to read:

'I am happy to inform you that the Government have approved Indian participation in this project through an NFDC partnered company, entering into co-production agreement with Indo-British Films.

'The necessary agreement for a specific co-production in this behalf will now need to be finalised between Indo-British Films and the Indian Company. We are asking the NFDC for further action in this matter. The Government have agreed to an overall financial commitment of the Indian party to the tune of 5 *Krores** and it is further agreed that there will be no restriction on the repatriation of rupee accruals. The proposed Indian company will also offer a guarantee for completion of the co-production.'

It was a marvellous document and I slept well on my journey home.

I brought back with me further observations on the script which had been assembled by our great protagonist, Sharada Prasad, the Prime Minister's adviser on all matters of public relations and communication. He had been a most tenacious ally in overcoming the log-jams that must baulk any project which requires such disparate governmental approval and co-operation. My personal debt to him is enormous, not only for his unparalleled assistance but also for his considerable friendship.

Jack reviewed all the suggested minor script modifications and most of them we incorporated. I had been told specifically they were merely recommendations and that there was no question of being obliged to make any alterations against our better judgement.

Shortly after my return, we engaged John Mollo as the film's

* *Krore*: ten million rupees.

His fast brings Gandhi to the brink of death.

other Costume Designer. His experience and specialist knowledge of military uniforms in particular proved invaluable, and together with Bhanu Athaiya he formed a most formidable complementary wardrobe team.

Production meetings headed by Mike or Terry were now held almost daily. A major consignment of three mobile catering vehicles, a refrigerator truck and a generator was shipped to Bombay. There were now only ten weeks to go before shooting started and time seemed to be slipping away at a frightening pace.

Our Casting Director was Susie Figgis who had acted as Assistant to Miriam Brickman on *A Bridge Too Far*. Her taste and knowledge proved impeccable. Her main problem with *Gandhi* was the vast number of very small parts which, nevertheless, had to be played by expert actors prepared to make the journey out to India for only a few days' work.

I was anxious to finalise Candice Bergen's contract to play Margaret Bourke-White, and Marti Baum's office in Los Angeles dealt with this for me. The next major character to be cast was the American reporter Walker who is based on an amalgam of Louis Fischer, Vincent Sheean and William Shirer. I had been enormously impressed by Martin Sheen's performance in *Apocalypse Now*, and I asked Marti if he could contact him. Marti sent him the script, and by return Martin Sheen replied that he would be honoured to appear in the production.

On 1 October I went back to India to check on the major construction work in progress with Stuart Craig and finalise the choice of the remaining locations. By now the production office was fully operational and Alex De Grunwald was established as British Production Manager, in tandem with Shama Habibullah.

There were some 150 Indians already employed on construction work and so far no catastrophes had occurred in terms of timetable. Our visit to Pune to make a final decision regarding the use of the Aga Khan Palace was an important one. Now a beautifully maintained museum, it looked somewhat too pristine but Stuart was convinced that with careful choice of camera angles and a certain amount of 'breaking down', we could re-establish the authentic atmosphere of the early 1940s.

Back in England after a ridiculously brief ten days travelling all over India, casting was again uppermost in my mind. The part of Charlie Andrews was an extremely telling one, and Susie had a marvellous idea. She had seen several reels of *Chariots of Fire*, in which one of the two leads was played by Ian Charleson. Hugh Hudson and David Puttnam, who were still in the process of editing, kindly allowed Mike, Susie and me to see an assembly of some forty minutes one Saturday morning in October. At the crack of dawn we went to the studios at Elstree and having seen the footage, walked out, utterly bowled over. Not only did Ian give a most remarkable performance (together with Ben Cross, who had played a tiny part in *A Bridge Too Far*), but the film itself rocked us back on our heels. All of us felt, even then, that *Chariots* could prove to be a prestigious success, not only at home but throughout the world.

Ian read the script, and to my delight agreed to play Charlie. I had also sent a copy to Edward Fox, asking him to play General Dyer, and of course to Johnny Mills, without whom I feel almost incapable of making a movie. Johnny generously and excitedly immediately agreed to play one of the Viceroys. Edward, however, had certain reservations about accepting the part of Dyer. It was a daunting task due to the painful nature of the sequence and required total conviction on the part of the actor concerned. In the final result, Edward's performance could not have been of a higher calibre.

Rohini had come over to England and like Ben was involved in a series of make-up and hair tests, more extensive than any in my experience.

Gandhi is confronted by the desperate Nahari (Om Puri), who has killed a Muslim baby in revenge for the murder of his son.
As news spreads that the Mahatma may die, peace gradually returns to Calcutta.

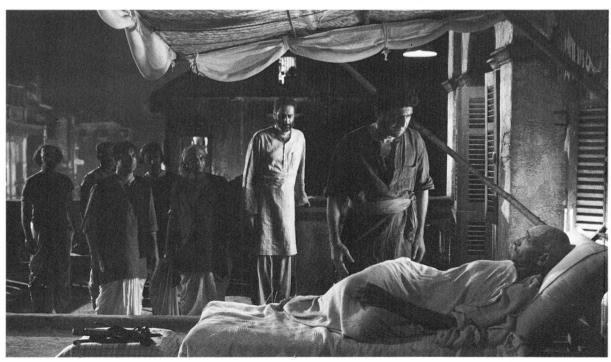

With Roshan Seth on a set in Bombay.

The one male character whose casting was still causing us great concern was Pandit Nehru. We finally tested four Indian actors, one of whom was Roshan Seth, who had trained in England at LAMDA but had subsequently given up acting and was editing a magazine in Delhi. We persuaded him to make a brief visit to London, and in terms of acting ability his performance was potentially outstanding. There were, however, certain limitations in regard to his physical acceptability as Pandit Nehru. These we worked on very hard with the costume and make-up departments, and when finally both we and he—which was perhaps more important—were convinced that he could carry it off, his contract was agreed.

It was while lunching after viewing Roshan's make-up test that Susie brought into the studio restaurant a red-headed young woman by the name of Geraldine James. I had seen her give two television performances of a vastly contrasting nature and had been greatly impressed. But the moment I clapped eyes on her in the flesh I knew she was the person to play Madeleine Slade. Mirabehn, as Bapu called her, was a British admiral's daughter who in 1925 gave up the comfort of her home in England, came to Gandhi's *ashram* and served him until his death.

We needed an exceptional stills cameraman for the picture in order to obtain a selection of photographs for world-wide publication. Frank Connor was the assistant stills man on *A Bridge Too Far*, and was my first choice for *Gandhi*. Many of the monochrome stills, and almost all the colour pictures in this book are the result of his skill, persistence and successful battle against the fine Indian dust which infiltrated daily every single piece of camera equipment.

There were still legal details that had to be finalised and my great concern was the tardiness with which the NFDC funds were being made available. We were left continually in a state of suspended animation, wondering whether we would be able to meet our commitments. A final meeting in London between Suresh and Malati Tambey Vaidya and our own advisers at one point reached what amounted to an impasse. I announced that we were due to start shooting in less than a month and that if the go-ahead was not given immediately without reservation there could be something equivalent to an international incident—a statement tinged as usual with my unfailing theatricality!

On other fronts, events were now moving at a lightning pace. Ben and Billy Williams left for Delhi during the last week in

October and I followed a few days later. There were now nearly 200 Indian crew working there, together with nearly thirty British, plus some twenty more ready to leave England. I remained in Delhi for only three days, just to have a final look at the locations and to urge and urge once more that the Ministry and the NFDC put in motion their various commitments.

Back in London, Susie was tying up last-minute casting, the most important of which was Sir John Gielgud's agreement to play Lord Irwin, one of the last Viceroys of India. Whether these sequences would be shot in India or England was not at that time decided. The one thing that was certain was that this remarkable actor would add immeasurably to the stature of the film.

A few days before I left to start shooting I had lunch with Dorothy Kothari and her son Raj. She was overjoyed and even found it hard to believe, I think, that at last her husband's dream was about to come to fruition. They were both very happy that Raj, who was a BBC television editor, was to join the cutting room staff on our return.

I finally departed for India exactly one week before we started shooting. There were inevitably the usual panics. A freight plane carrying all our equipment made a forced landing in Paris. There had also been a moment of crisis when the production department led by Terry asked me to consider a postponement or even the possible cancellation of the film because facilities which had been promised and undertakings which had been given were just not forthcoming. These were the inevitable result of bureaucracy which would apply in any country in the world, though immensely frustrating for those who had to cope with them. However, in the nick of time permissions were granted, frayed nerves soothed and all was well. Everything and everybody seemed to have arrived, and after a last-minute scrambled tour around the locations, construction and wardrobe departments, shooting was set to begin on 26 November 1980.

9

Together with the crew I left the Ashok Hotel at 6.30 a.m., for the Batra stone works in Sikanderpura Ghasi village about twenty-five miles west of Delhi. Shortly after the arrival of Ben Kingsley and the other actors, following a simple ceremony called *muhurat*, in which a Hindu priest blesses the camera, we started work.

The scene was meant to be a Southern African mine at which the young Gandhi led one of his initial protest demonstrations. This was quite complicated; we were using for the first time the Louma crane, which under the appropriate circumstances permits one to devise shots encompassing 360° which are impossible with the standard equipment. It was the first of 121 days in India, many of which, with the addition of production meetings—sometimes even on the one weekly rest day—rarely finished before 11 p.m. I thought in anticipation that I would be very apprehensive, but that didn't prove to be the case. There were so many practical problems—we had a crowd of approximately three hundred, together with a troop of mounted police—that I was too preoccupied for first-day nerves. Knowing that we were working from the best possible script helped too. A large part of film-making is a matter of team work, but the writer, without whom there can be no movie, works to a great extent in solitude. The screenplay that Jack Briley finally produced could not, in my opinion, have been surpassed. His writing was taut, elegant, moving, humorous and hugely informed, centred always on Gandhiji himself, with an unflagging narrative drive.

Ben as ever arrived promptly on the set. He looked marvellous, full of confidence and prepared for the arduous job that lay ahead. He had read all the books on Gandhiji we were able to give him and had visited every locale where Bapu had spent any significant part of his life. His height was almost identical with Gandhiji's. However, one had to admit he was not as thin! But by eating prescribed vegetarian food he had lost some seventeen pounds

Mingling with the crowd assembling in the gardens of Birla House to hear the Mahatma conduct evening prayers is the young Hindu fanatic Nathuram Godse (Harsh Nayar).

before we began shooting. With the aid of a tutor, he learned to spin cotton thread on two different types of *charka** and within a very short space of time he was an adept.

To emulate Gandhiji's supple physical movements, he devoted ninety minutes to yoga every evening. His hotel room became a sort of shrine; on one wall there were huge blow-ups of Bapu in movement and on the other, equally magnified pictures of the Mahatma's mobile face. Chairs were replaced by straw-filled mattresses surrounded by bolsters, and he slept on a cot.

The extent of his personal magnetism was soon demonstrated. Our second key sequence was filmed in a massive convention tent with a crowd of over thirteen hundred. Ben was called upon to address them—supposedly after he had returned to India in 1915—speaking of the path he believed they must follow to gain Independence. He was as usual word-perfect, and at the conclusion of the speech, which ran for several minutes, he was greeted by thunderous applause from crew and crowd alike.

The most important set to be constructed in India was the *ashram*, on the bank of a river some forty minutes' drive from our hotel. Fortunately, we were able to build it early enough to allow for proper weathering. There was even sufficient time to allow for the growth of appropriate crops in the surrounding fields. The one mishap which occurred was during the monsoon, when the river became so swollen that part of the bank where we were constructing the outer buildings of the *ashram* was swept away, leaving Bapu's shade tree, which was to have been the focal point of his daily prayer meetings, high and dry in the middle of the river—though still the haunt of kingfishers and emerald green parakeets.

During our ten weeks' shooting in and around Delhi the majority of our time was spent at the *ashram*. It had an extraordinary atmosphere of serenity and the effect on the entire crew was remarkable. It engendered a feeling of gentleness and understanding which did much, I think, to bond the unit together as an entity.

We did not have an easy time with the press from the word go. On the first occasion they were invited to watch the shooting Ben was greatly disturbed by a number of the questions fired at him. One woman actually asked if it was true that he had begun his film career in pornographic movies! There seemed to be a faction which was determined to be destructive. Nevertheless,

* *Charka*: a wooden spinning-wheel.

Prakash (Prabhakar Patankar), one of the principal conspirators at Birla House on 30 January 1948.

At the ashram *with screenwriter Jack Briley and Bapu's marooned shade tree.*

professional that he is, Ben overcame this hurdle and we all learned to allow our experienced public relations department to take the brunt of the onslaught.

The first principal Indian player on the set was Amrish Puri. He exemplified the courtesy and professionalism displayed without exception by all the Indian artists. The work tempo in India, with the actors engaged on as many as twenty-five films concurrently and therefore having constantly to readjust themselves in relation to a particular character which perhaps they have not played for some weeks, results of necessity in evident technical efficiency. The principal problem facing me as director was consequently to persuade them that there was really sufficient time to consider and adjust their character's involvement in a particular scene and that the time taken would be amply justified by the end result.

In our third week we faced a crowd of over 2,000. It was the occasion when Rohini made her first appearance. Both she and I were, I know, a little apprehensive, but she managed it magnificently, delivering a speech in impeccable English. As with Ben, she, too, had disciplined herself. She, too, had learned to spin. She, too, had read everything she could lay her hands on about Kasturba. But in addition, she had studied her English dialogue meticulously. As a Marathi theatre actress she used English very little, but by the end of the film she was conversing fluently with all of us.

We used the gardens of Teen Murti, Pandit Nehru's house in Delhi, which is now a museum and library dedicated to his life's work, for a scene involving one of the Viceroys. It was the first time that we shot the totally different, pampered atmosphere of the Raj and authenticity was of paramount importance. Johnny Mills played the Viceroy—perfectly, of course. He was the first guest star to appear and had with him Bernard Hepton, Nigel Hawthorne and James Cossins. The wardrobe department had done us proud, and the splendour and pomp of the occasion was, I think, captured very successfully.

Shooting at Rashtrapati Bhavan, formerly the Viceregal palace, caused us some problems. There were several sequences which we had hoped to stage inside, together with one very dramatic scene outside when Gandhi is summoned to see Lord Irwin prior to the 1931 Conference. Rani spent day after day attempting to obtain the formal approval of the President, Shri Sanjiva Reddy, and finally gained permission to use the exterior. We arrived at 6.30 a.m. in order to avoid both visitors and the interference of traffic. During winter an early morning mist sometimes enshrouds Delhi and on the first occasion we lined up a massive rostrum and the Louma crane, although we shot the scene, we knew almost certainly that our efforts were in vain. Our worst fears were borne out and we had to retake the sequence, all the approvals having to be obtained anew, some weeks later.

The film begins in the gardens of Birla House, the actual place of Mahatma Gandhi's assassination. We spent a week working there, and were conscious of the very special permission that had been granted. The lawn where the Mahatma was killed is treated

8 September 1982: Shri Zaid Singh, the newly-elected President of India, accepts an invitation to be guest of honour at the film's world première in New Delhi on 30 November.

with the utmost respect, and, as was expected of us, the entire crew worked without shoes, as did the crowd.

The impact on those present when we actually filmed the moment of the Mahatma's death was extraordinary. I well remember Ben shaking like a leaf and telling me, as we walked back to his little caravan for a rest, that it was the most awesome experience he had ever undergone.

The part of his assassin, Nathuram Godse, was played by an actor named Harsh Nayar, who is, ironically, a nephew of Pyarelal Nayar, Gandhi's biographer. He looks in broad facial features not unlike Godse himself. I cast him for his eyes: they were almost unblinking. He, too, of course, found the occasion profoundly disturbing and prepared himself for the moment he would have to fire the gun by never talking to Ben beforehand, or even—if he could avoid it—being in his presence.

Our next sequence was, with perhaps the exception of the assassination, the most traumatic in the entire film. Indeed it is one of the most dramatic moments in Indian history; the Jallianwala Bagh massacre in the Sikh capital city of Amritsar. In fact, we shot all but the approach through the streets, in Delhi, since the journey up to the north-west of India would have been completely impractical in terms of the time required for the whole unit to travel. Consequently, the make-up and wardrobe departments were presented with an enormous task; all the Sikhs are bearded, and, in 1919 they all wore a very specific costume. We called a crowd of several thousand. This incident meant a great deal to the Indians taking part, and the reality they brought to this particular episode—in which hundreds were either killed or wounded—was extraordinary. Chalkie White had spent many days with the officers commanding the Gurkhas and the Balluchis, who, in the film, were under the command of General Dyer, played by Edward Fox. I think much of the impact of the sequence, as far as the Indian crowd was concerned and therefore on the screen, stemmed from the authenticity of these troops.

One of the problems for the Art Department was trains. They were the only linking network throughout India during the period of our story, but then of course they were steam trains, not diesel, and they ran on different gauges from most of those which operate today. This situation applied to Southern Africa as well and a certain number therefore had to be re-rigged both inside and out. The most telling scene was I suppose the one in which young Gandhi was thrown off a train because he was

206

sitting in a first-class carriage. Travelling up and down the line, with the complication of clearing all other traffic from sections of track, was very time-consuming. But nowadays, with so much documentary film available both in the cinema and on television, such sequences only have the ring of truth when they are shot in the actual setting.

The entire Southern Africa segment of the script was shot in India. We were granted permission by the Government to film in Hyderabad House, which the Art Department converted into a palatial office for the scene between Gandhi and General Smuts. Another of Susie's marvellous ideas was to suggest that we should ask the celebrated South African playwright and actor, Athol Fugard, to play Smuts. To my great pleasure, he agreed and consequently brought not only authenticity to the General's accent, but also graced the film with a fine performance.

Whilst in India, Sheila and I invited Indiraji for dinner. With the minimum of security, she arrived at the Ashok very privately in her little white Ambassador car. We showed her some of the stills that had been taken so far and, during the evening, a number

Margaret Bourke-White captures Gandhi's image for the last time at Birla House. Still weak from fasting, he is supported by Abha (Nina Gupta) and Manu (Supriya Pathak), his two great-nieces who have cared for him, together with Mirabehn, since Kasturba's death.

of the crew came in to meet her. She stayed quite late and amazed many by her familiarity with the techniques of film-making. Shortly afterwards, accompanied by her family, she came to watch us working at Hyderabad House.

During the last few days in January, we were due to shoot inside the Viceroy's palace, and in requesting permission, we were not as fortunate as previously. Whereas the President had been content that we should film outside, he did not think it appropriate that we should use the interior of Rashtrapati Bhavan. The result was that the Speaker of the Lok Sabha, with the knowledge of the Prime Minister, gave approval for us to work in a part of the Lutyens buildings simulating the areas needed for the scenes involving Lord Mountbatten as the final Viceroy of India.

The largest set piece in the whole picture was the staging of the Mahatma's funeral, which we shot thirty-three years to the day after the actual event, on 31 January 1981.

Under David Tomblin's overall command, with the detail being supervised by Chalkie White, we planned it meticulously. We appealed to the public to come and support us and appear as mourners. We flew out additional camera crews from England and augmented the Indian crews that were already working with the first and second units. There were eleven separate camera positions filming the whole cortège as it moved slowly from Rashtrapati Bhavan down Rajpath towards India Gate.

The organisation of huge crowds, whether on this occasion or in the Jallianwala Bagh, or the sequence at Motihari station, requires both discipline and tactical ability. Wardrobe and make-up begin working at two or three in the morning. Large-scale transportation, kitchens, additional special catering, all have to be organised, and at the end of the day, those who are specifically employed must, of course, be paid. It was a massive operation, and one which, if not undertaken in terms of a military exercise, could result in chaos. In this particular instance, the requirements were even more precise, since each person involved in the actual cortège had to be dressed in correct historical costume, and by the end of the morning—which was the length of time we were permitted to close Rajpath—the entire sequence had to be completed.

The cortège itself was made up of 1,060 people, surrounded by a further 1,000 of specifically cast crowd. There was a guard of honour comprising 3,000 Home Guard, 500 members of the

ON FOLLOWING PAGE
Mahatma Gandhi leaves his quarters at Birla House, New Delhi, to conduct prayers in the garden.

OPPOSITE
With Indiraji on the day she watched us filming at Hyderabad House.

My partner, Mike Stanley-Evans, in action at our press conference in Bombay.

Gandhi Peace Movement, 30,000 spectators whom we had brought to the site in organised transports, together with a further 50,000 from the country areas who also made the journey in special buses. There was an additional crowd of carefully selected 'front liners' numbering some 9,000 and, as we put on our call sheet, 250,000 'invited guests', who had inevitably to make their own arrangements.

There was debate in the very early hours of the morning as to how effective our appeal had been. Some newspapers suggested that we only had a mere 20,000 people present. However, since we ourselves had been responsible for an attendance approaching 100,000 it seemed to us that the estimates were somewhat wide of the mark. When asked, the police decreed that the crowd was somewhere between 250,000 and 350,000. In any event, the day passed without any problem, and none of the forecast demonstrations by those supposedly opposed to the film materialised.

As far as camera was concerned, the whole sequence was in the charge of Ronnie Taylor. Billy Williams was unwell for part of shooting and, when he had to return to England, Ronnie took his place. Ronnie was Camera Operator on *Lovely War* and was now a Lighting Cameraman in his own right. He photographed a considerable portion of the film and I am certain that Billy would agree that he did a magnificent job. As might have been expected, the unit was exhausted that Saturday night. It marked, however, the completion of our shooting in the Delhi area.

The following day, the massive operation of moving the entire crew with all its equipment, including the huge wardrobe and kitchens and heavy transport, half-way across India to Bombay had to begin. Most of the crew moved there directly by rail and road and air; but a smaller unit comprising Ben and Martin Sheen, together with camera and sound crews, make-up, props, electricians and stand-bys, with myself and an assistant went to Porbandar.

Porbandar is Gandhi's birthplace and we had one scene which I wished to film there if humanly possible. It was vital that it was completed within the one and a half days scheduled. If we failed, we would have to abandon shooting the sequence there since we could not afford to keep the main unit idle in Bombay. By a miracle the weather was ideal; the sunset was one we might have prayed for and the two actors were perfection. Not once, in a lengthy exchange of dialogue, did either of them fluff one word

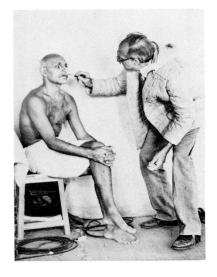

Tom Smith adds a finishing touch to Ben's make-up just before a take.

Second unit Director/Cameraman, Govind Nihalani.

and by good luck and great skill we achieved everything we needed within three and a half hours. This meant that we had time to spare for a look around the town and a visit to Gandhiji's birthplace—a luxury we never dreamt would be possible.

We had several vital sequences to shoot in Bombay. The first was the final protest undertaken by the Congress Party members during the 1930 campaign at the Dharasana salt works. It was witnessed by Martin Sheen as Walker and Richard Griffiths who had now joined us to play Collins, the London *Times* reporter. Logistically, it was extremely difficult to shoot, since it had to be staged on the only road linking two villages and consequently, after each camera set-up, we had to suspend filming to allow the considerable build-up of traffic and pedestrians to go about their daily business. The scene was, I think, as moving as any in the script and, taken with the rest of his part, it affected Martin deeply. As a result, before he returned home to the States he told Mike and me that he wished his entire salary to go to charity, a large portion of which he donated to Mother Teresa in Calcutta. This had also been the reaction of Edward Fox and so, with some significantly smaller contributions from Mike and myself, Martin and Edward's salaries went to the charities of their choice.

The second major sequence was in the port of Bombay where we needed a vessel of the type in use in 1915, moored at a particular quay. Luckily we were able to use the P & O liner *MS Dwarka*, still in service between India and the Gulf States. However, her sailing schedule meant that if we failed to film what we needed in the allotted time, we would find ourselves sans ship. The gods, however, were thoughtfully with us, and we completed our work before she had to leave.

213

In quick succession, at almost point blank range, Godse fires three shots that end the life of the Mahatma.

RIGHT
Mahatma Gandhi sinks to the ground. His last words, 'O God,' are those he always hoped would be on his lips when he died.

The final scenes to be staged in Bombay involved the riots resulting in Gandhiji's fast which factually took place in Calcutta. They were shot in a densely populated district both during the day and throughout the night. Undoubtedly we caused the local populace considerable inconvenience with our myriad lamps and all the noise that night shooting entails.

Filming throughout the night is a very debilitating experience and the demands on Ben's concentration and skill were at their height. Needless to say, however, he rose to the challenge as did Om Puri, the highly praised young actor who plays a vital part in the penultimate scene. It was during this period that there occurred the one tragedy of our 26-week schedule. The huge crowds wanting to watch us became at times almost uncontrollable and people clambered all over the adjoining buildings in order to obtain a better view. Sadly, one evening a young boy was killed as the wall on which he was perched collapsed. It caused all of us great distress, and we were only slightly comforted in that the fatality was not directly of our making.

On Monday, 16 March the unit moved to Pune where our principal work was to be within the Aga Khan Palace. We shot there for five days. The Trustees of the Palace, which is now a museum, having been given to the nation by the present Aga

Khan, had requested us to make certain minor revisions to several of the scenes. We agreed to them all with one exception and had an understanding that we would shoot the single line they felt unable to accept in its original form and in an amended version of their choice. When the film was completed we undertook to show them both alternatives and they would be at liberty to make the final choice.

Fanned by the 'Committee to Oppose (the) Feature Film on Gandhiji', there was a fair amount of hysteria nominally led by the ex-Prime Minister, Morarji Desai. Several newspapers reported that he would embark on a fast if the amendments that had been asked for were not incorporated in the script. It was all quite ludicrous, since from the word go we had most willingly given the necessary undertakings.

A panoramic view of the unit preparing for work showing the restaurant tents, and an array of the vehicles needed for transport, make-up, hair, sound, camera, props, wardrobe, dressing rooms—and the ladies' and gents' indispensable 'honey wagons'.

Having completed the remaining sequences in Pune, including the Southern African mosque scene involving the burning of passes and the meeting of protest in the Imperial Theatre, we moved to Patna in Bihar on April 3.

It was in Patna that we shot the Champaran indigo farmers' revolt not far from where it actually took place. This provided Gandhi with his first public opportunity to oppose British authority in India. We made the considerable journey up to the North East since I was very anxious to film the quite different facial structures and skin colour indigenous to that part of the country. I also wanted to show the expressions of those who had, in their own lives, known poverty. The opening shots were set against a background of some fifteen thousand people. Dominic Guard and Bernard Hill, who had only the day before flown out from England, must have undergone something of the experience that faced the actual young British troops who had to deal with such circumstances during the Raj.

Having completed the work in Patna within eight days, we moved to our final location across India to Udaipur where the temperature was constantly in the hundreds. We spent the greater part of our time there on the overcrowded roofs of steam trains, speeding along the only available stretch of track we could find with the correct locomotive on the correct terrain against a background of appropriate countryside.

I have already compared filming with military manoeuvres, and would further the analogy by agreeing with Napoleon that an army marches on its stomach. Throughout the entire shooting period in India, no matter how remote or inaccessible the setting, Phil Hobbs's Location Caterers, together with a team of Indian colleagues, were always in advance of the troops. No matter how early the call, we would arrive to find vast, brightly coloured marquees, known as *shamianas*, already erected so that we could eat in shade. Both Indian and English menus were on offer to every member of the unit. We breakfasted, lunched and sometimes supped right royally and the fact that the crew remained remarkably fit in spite of every tropical pitfall, is due to Phil and his team's fastidiousness over every aspect of hygiene— let alone their ability to serve up roast beef and Yorkshire pudding in the middle of nowhere!

The British unit finally started to move back to London via Bombay and Delhi on 17 April.

There had, inevitably, been problems between some members of the Indian and British crews. But, in my honest opinion, they were no more than might occur amongst any unit emanating from one country suddenly transported into alien circumstances and living cheek by jowl for a period in excess of six months with local film-makers. There was never in any of our minds a thought that the Indian crew should not be treated as properly and understandingly as the British. That I am sure was also the view of Rani Dube—who, as it were, sat in the middle—and of Suresh Jindal and Shama Habibullah who led the Indian contingent. National customs, differing accommodation requirements, total-ly different eating habits, all lead to rumours and potential unrest and it would be foolish, indeed dishonest, to deny that there was not a certain friction. However, none of it was fundamental and, as the British crew left, the airports were crowded with Indian friends and colleagues who came to say *au revoir* and wish us a speedy return. Few faces were free of tears and many of the crew have, in fact, already been back to India for holidays. I was, of course, familiar with the British crew; however, I would wish to state categorically that the effort and application shown by the

ON FOLLOWING PAGE
Mahatma Gandhi's state funeral in Delhi. His body lies surrounded by flowers on a carriage escorted by men of the Indian Army, Navy and Air Force. It is escorted by a guard of servicemen and throngs of mourners, while vast crowds line the route to pay their final homage.

Indian members of the unit in achieving a tight shooting schedule on time, with but few compromises, was a remarkable accomplishment. This was greatly aided by the singular contribution of the second unit under the direction of Govind Nihalani. The sequences to which they contributed were enormously strengthened by their input and they must share, in real terms, whatever success the film may achieve.

Together with a number of the key technicians we left Delhi on the night of 18 April. There was no Air India flight—the airline we had used almost without exception—and so we returned to England on Pan Am. It was an unnerving experience. We had been in India so long that walking into an aircraft to be greeted by American accents, suddenly we were no longer 'at home'. All that remained of India were the garlands which had been lovingly placed around our necks in farewell.

It was odd to be back in the studios at Shepperton: old-fashioned in a way. The true settings in which we had worked for so long contributed great authenticity to the film and we now had to be certain that the fabricated sets, both in and out of the studios, did not erode that reality.

We had various English exteriors to shoot: Kingsley Hall in the East End of London, the Lancashire cotton mills and Buckingham Palace. But there were also two principal sequences involving Sir John Gielgud and Trevor Howard. Johnnie G. playing Lord Irwin was joined, as his staff, by a group of distinguished actors, Ian Bannen, Michael Bryant, Bernard Horsfall and Richard Leech. They created an atmosphere

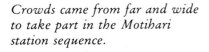

Crowds came from far and wide to take part in the Motihari station sequence.

intrinsically English and correct, which at once achieved the particular style which now permeates the scene.

The other important sequence was staged in the old town hall at Staines, Middlesex, reconstructed and dressed as a courtroom of the 1920s in India. Historically, the occasion was known as 'the Great Trial' presided over by Judge Broomfield. He was played by Trevor Howard with Sir John Clements as the Advocate General. It was a vital scene as far as I was concerned. I hoped that it would encapsulate in its brief but dramatic placing all that was best in the administration, and compassionate understanding of British rule in India. Needless to say, Trevor managed to convey this superbly.

The final shot in the schedule was set outside No. 10 Downing Street where Ben, dressed in his *dhoti* with his staff in hand, bade farewell to Prime Minister Ramsay MacDonald at the conclusion of the abortive 1931 Conference.

We finished filming on Sunday, 10 May, on our 126th day. We had shot approximately three and a quarter hours of screen time at a daily average of one minute twenty-nine seconds, exposing five hundred and twenty-five thousand, one hundred and fifty feet of film stock.

Jake Eberts was certainly enormously relieved that we were all back safe and sound and that the film had been completed within its budget. It had been a major show of faith on his part and that of Goldcrest that had allowed us to keep going throughout the various crises in the financing of the production. On several hair-raising occasions the money had almost run out and all that we retained were funds to pay our existing contractual commitments and get the crew back to England. During one particular period when twenty per cent of the film's finance evaporated into thin air, James Lee flew out to India on a lightning visit to assess the situation on the spot and went back, recommending to the board of Pearson Longman that they should cover the shortfall. Another person who offered help in a moment of crisis was Sydney Samuelson whose company is the major supplier of camera and lighting equipment. Sydney telexed me in Pune, volunteering to defer all outstanding and future hire charges—which form a substantial part of any budget—until *Gandhi* moved into profit. Such faith and friendship is pretty rare.

Johnnie Bloom and Chris Ridsdale had done a mammoth job in assembling a number of important sequences. We worked without respite, putting together in a viewable condition about

OPPOSITE
The funeral cortège.

two hours of film and Marti Baum flew over from LA in order to see it with Johnny Redway.

At that time in July 1981 we had no distributor and Jake was very anxious to secure a return on part of the vast sums which Goldcrest now had invested in the production. Since the film had cost approximately $22 million it was obvious that the investors would want the film to be shown as soon as possible after its completion in order to avoid unnecessary additional interest charges. I was, however, very conscious that a considerable marketing operation had to be set in train prior to the opening in order to create an awareness of the film's subject matter, scale and setting amongst the public at large. This would be more than mere advertising and publicity: I believed a major campaign was essential and without it the film might well founder.

We agreed, therefore, on Marti's advice, to take a gamble. We decided to show the two hours of film to all the principal American distributors in the hope of receiving an acceptable offer from one of them, permitting the whole machinery of marketing and promotion to begin before the post-production work was finally completed.

As a result Jake and I together with Pedro Tietelbaum, our adviser in distribution matters at that time, left for the States.

Every major distributor made an offer. Some of them I knew, some I had never met before. However, ultimately the choice appeared to reside between Paramount, Warner Brothers and Columbia. I was greatly touched that Charles Bludhorn, the Chairman of Gulf and Western, Paramount's parent company, made an exception in viewing the film at this early stage when normally he left such matters to the President of Paramount Pictures, Barry Diller, and the Head of Production, Michael Eisener. We ran the footage in a large viewing room in a theatre which would normally hold two hundred. At the end of the running Charlie in his usual generous way said, 'Dickie, I'm proud of you, Paramount must have this film.'

As things turned out a deal was not concluded with Paramount, despite long meetings with Charlie and a number of his executives. The reason was that although Paramount unquestionably had as good a domestic distribution organisation headed by Frank Mancuso as existed in the United States, their international arrangements were not, in my judgement, anything like as satisfactory. This view was subsequently confirmed by the fact that having been specifically asked to show the film to their

executives in London we received a very indifferent reaction, scarcely more than a polite thank you.

Warner Brothers, with whom I had previously had negotiations, were immensely enthusiastic—particularly Terry Semel and Bob Shapiro.

However, the reaction that topped them all was that of Columbia. Marti had always wanted us to end up with them and had arranged for the Chairman and Chief Executive, Frank Price, the President of Marketing, Marvin Antonowsky, and Head of Production, John Veitch, to see the picture. At the conclusion of the running, Frank asked Jake, Pedro and me if we would remain in the theatre for ten minutes or so. We were then invited to Frank's office where he said that to all intents and purposes Columbia were prepared to outbid any other offer that we might receive. As far as they were concerned it was one of the most important pictures with which they had ever had the opportunity of being involved and they very much wanted the foreign division of Columbia to see it if we were willing to return to London via New York. Of course we agreed, and on arrival showed the film to their principal staff including the Vice-President, David Matalon, and a friend of many years standing, the President of Columbia Pictures International, Pat Williamson.

Their reaction exactly matched that of their colleagues on the Coast. Pat and David both said that they wished to take the film for the rest of the world including India. Therefore despite further conversations with Charlie we finally agreed a contract with Columbia. The fact that the deal covered the whole world with all the resultant advantages of planning an overall promotional concept was without doubt the deciding factor.

I had to get back to London immediately in order to take up my responsibilities as Deputy Chairman of the new Channel 4 Television Company. I had been appointed before the commencement of shooting but undertaken to so arrange my commitments that I would be available for meetings on completion of the actual filming. We returned to Los Angeles and New York briefly to finalise our discussions with Columbia and present our broad concepts of promotion in relation to the stills and publicity material that had been assembled during shooting. This was Diana Hawkins's responsibility and several of those present said that it was the most impressive presentation they had ever witnessed.

Having now seen the overall shape the film was taking, the

music requirements were beginning to formulate in my mind. It had always been my hope that our timetable would allow Pandit Ravi Shankar to be the composer. However, I felt that it would be impossible for him to deal with the entire score, since I also wanted parts of the music to reflect authentically the sound of the British Raj in all its splendour. I therefore wished to engage a British composer to work with him.

Rani and I left for India in the middle of October. Closeted in a tiny little projection room in studios outside Bombay, we showed Ravi the first rough assembly of the entire picture. His reaction could not have been more rewarding. He was deeply affected by the film and said he would be delighted to be involved. We discussed the broad strategies that might achieve what was bound to be a most complicated musical concept. I told him I had in mind a young composer in England who had worked primarily in theatre and television, named George Fenton. Once again, as with Ben, it was through my son Michael that I came to know of George's work. George paid two visits to India to spend time with Ravi working on the score, and came back to London very excited by the potential that both believed existed.

On 25 November Frank Price, Marvin Antonowsky, Pat Williamson and David Matalon all flew to London in order to announce at a press conference that Columbia had acquired worldwide distribution rights in the picture. Frank stated that *Gandhi* represented the Company's biggest ever opening commitment in securing worldwide distribution rights for any film.

'The High Command.' For the long shots, in order to blend with servicemen escorting the cortège (right to left) Mike (Chalkie) White, Steve Lanning, Roy Button and I wore military uniform regardless of our haircuts.

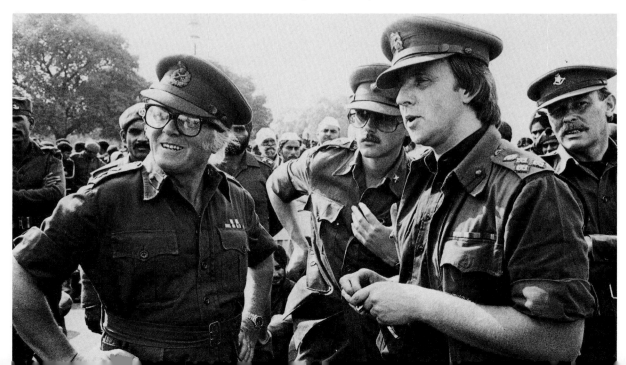

Gandhi's body is shrouded in flowers on its journey to the funeral pyre. Only his face is visible to the masses who mourn him on the route.

Anyone writing about film production tends almost inevitably to short-change the editing period. It is, in fact, almost as exciting and rewarding as the actual shooting. But unless one goes into the minutiae, it is a process which is well nigh impossible to describe. Suffice it to say that one can spend days and days with the editor working on the smaller nuances to rebalance a sequence which might, in the end, run for no more than a minute and a half. Immense technical skill is required as far as the editor is concerned; however, overriding all else is his sense of taste and judgement.

I have not encountered a finer editor anywhere in the world than Johnnie Bloom. His application to the job and his creativity in my opinion are without parallel and much credit for the film that audiences will see is due to him.

There were two other key technicians who came into their own during the post-production phase, Jonathan Bates, the Dubbing Editor, and Gerry Humphries, the Dubbing Mixer. Jonathan creates the soundtrack, including every imaginable sound effect, in addition to ensuring that each line of dialogue is not only intelligible but also properly free of any incongruous or extraneous sound. This often means going through a process of re-recording the dialogue with the inevitable problem of matching each minute lip movement. Gerry's task, seated with his two aides at a giant electronic console is to mix together just the right balance of all the tracks, including the music. Both are masters of their respective crafts.

Johnnie Bloom had supplied Ravi and George with the precise footages for the timing of the score. We had been through the film meticulously, deciding where and how the music should contribute. The decision as to the amount that might be most effective is a very delicate one—I personally tend to favour less rather than more. However, in this particular film, as far as exhibition in India is concerned, we may well have to increase the amount of music since it forms a great part of what audiences expect from a visit to the cinema. George and Ravi wrote separately, finally coming together early in the New Year to complete their work and hand over their scores for copying.

Amongst those attending the cremation of Mahatma Gandhi on 31 January 1948 are Lady Louis Mountbatten, Lord Louis Mountbatten, Maulana Azad, Pandit Nehru and Sardar Patel.

Gandhi with the two great-nieces he called 'my walking sticks', Manu and Abha. An archive photograph.

The complexities that we had set ourselves were considerable. Obviously, the Wren Orchestra would play from manuscripts under George Fenton's baton. The Indians neither worked from a score, nor of course, was their music conceived in Western terms, much of it being initially improvised. However, since it was to blend with a symphony orchestra, it had to be prescribed to a greater degree than would normally have been their custom. The result was that recording the music took considerably longer than usual.

A group of distinguished Indian musicians arrived in England during the second week in January 1982, many of them to see for the first time a blanket of snow which was covering the country. One of the difficulties immediately apparent was that the temperature in the recording studios had to be built up to one that was acceptable as far as they were concerned. This was to help their manual dexterity and to ensure that the actual sound of the instruments was not detrimentally affected. Some tones of which the instruments were capable were being heard almost for the first time in a Western recording studio, and certainly in the expertise displayed by the various musicians the occasion was unique. The recording took seven days to complete but everyone who came to the CTS studios at Wembley to listen felt that the ultimate result, achieved without compromise, was worth all the effort.

The dubbing of the final soundtrack was now well under way and at last, slowly, reel by reel, we heard what the end result was to be. We returned to India to show what amounted to the final version to various authorities and personalities who were entitled to see it. The reaction seemed universally favourable. The Prime Minister has since been generous enough to state publicly that, 'The film has captured the spirit of Gandhiji.'

The one sadness expressed by certain people in India was that a number of the major political figures involved in Indian history during the first half of the twentieth century were not depicted. This reaction, needless to say, we had anticipated, and it was necessary once more to explain that we were not telling the story of the Indian Independence struggle or even that of the Congress Party—we were telling the story of Mahatma Gandhi.

There were several showings which had to be given for both moral and legal reasons, one of which was for the Trustees of the Aga Khan Palace. Mr R. R. Diwakar, a past Minister of Information and Broadcasting, who was now in his eighty-seventh year, travelled from the south of India to Delhi in order to see the film that he had first heard of almost twenty years before when Moti and I went to see him. He, together with other officials of the Trust, had the right to approve or not approve the alternatives of one particular scene shot in the Palace. He found the film, he said, deeply moving but he was not content that in India it should contain the scripted line of dialogue and so I agreed to remove it. He expressly added, however, that he would not presume to bring pressure to bear as far as any other country was concerned. I asked him if the omission of certain aspects of Gandhi's life, certain episodes in Indian history, or certain personalities involved in the struggle for Independence was a matter of distress to him. After a pause, he replied quietly, 'What you have done is a work of art. One would not attempt to dictate the number of feathers Picasso might choose to display on a dove's wing.' I have to admit not only to being very touched but flattered too—no matter how extravagant the compliment!

The long operation of grading the picture now began, and both Billy Williams and Ronnie Taylor spent considerable time at Technicolor with me reaching final conclusions on the hues and densities of each sequence. As soon as this work was well under way I had to return to Bombay to start work on the Hindi dub, the ultimate process to be undergone before finally handing the film over to Columbia. I had hoped that it might be finished within a six-week period as far as the artists were concerned. However, it proved infinitely more difficult than I had anticipated, and took months rather than weeks to complete. It is an extremely difficult and trying process and if it succeeds, as I believe it will, the credit must go to Vinod Sharma and Kamlakar Datey who masterminded the whole operation.

On Sunday morning, 20 June, at the Odeon Leicester Square we held the unit showing. Some 1,500 people came: it was the first occasion upon which a sizeable audience had seen the picture, and many of them were responsible for the film eventually reaching the screen. I would have given almost anything for Moti to have been there. I hope he would have approved.

As we were leaving the theatre, one of the construction boys and his family came over.

'Tell you what, Guv, I'd go back and do the whole bloody lot again if you asked me to. It's all right!' he said.

I can only hope that others who see the film will feel the same way.

ON FOLLOWING PAGE
Mahatma Gandhi's ashes are consigned to the sacred waters of the River Ganges and the world mourns his passing.

The sum total of Gandhi's worldly goods at the time of his death. An archive photograph.

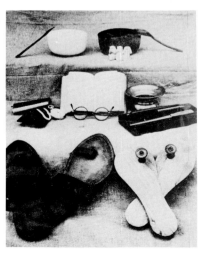

ACKNOWLEDGEMENTS

Since completing this book, two major changes have taken place at the Ministry of Information and Broadcasting in New Delhi. Mr S. B. Lal has been appointed Secretary and Mr N. K. P. Salve the Minister. Both have continued the kind co-operation of their predecessors and I would like to express my thanks to them.

Nothing of any material significance takes place at Beaver Lodge without the unstinting assistance of Leonard Clark, Gladys Barnes and Laurence Coughlan. We have worked together for many years and I value their loyalty enormously.

The production would never have come to fruition without the invaluable help of our army of legal advisers, and I would wish to thank them all: Claude E. Fielding, Sir John Terry, Eban Faizullabhoy, Simon Olswang, Elizabeth Matthews and Selwyn Remington.

When Max Reinhardt, the Chairman of The Bodley Head, was intemperate enough to invite me to put pen to paper, he comforted me with the information that he would ask one of his senior editors to guide my hand. Jill Black has always been extraordinarily helpful and infinitely patient, despite the headaches that I am sure I have given her, and I thank her very much. I must also express my gratitude to Sarah Laffey, who worked with such loving care on the book's design.

Finally, the book would not have reached the printers at all had it not been for Diana Hawkins who has not only attempted to ensure that the text is reasonably literate, but has, by an amalgam of bullying and cajolery, kept my nose to the grindstone. I am greatly in her debt.

RICHARD ATTENBOROUGH
Beaver Lodge, Richmond, October 1982

The photographs in this book appear by kind permission of Lotte Weitner-Graf, page 8, Sir Peter Saunders, page 57, Joe Cocks, page 193, Sheila Attenborough, page 153, Frank Connor and Pablo Bartholomew or are in the possession of the author. All archive pictures are by courtesy of the Gandhi Museum, Delhi.

On the titles of the film the producers express their profound gratitude for incalculable assistance given to them by those mentioned below: I would like to reiterate those thanks:

The Ministry of Information and Broadcasting
and
The Ministries and Departments of the Government of India involved with the production

The Governments of the Indian States in which filming took place

The Custodians and Trustees of the locations used for shooting

The Gandhi National Museum
and
The Navajivan Trust for allowing the use of its copyright material in the works of Mahatma Gandhi

THE CAST

Mahatma Gandhi : **Ben Kingsley**
Margaret Bourke-White : **Candice Bergen**
General Dyer : **Edward Fox**
Lord Irwin : **John Gielgud**
Judge Broomfield : **Trevor Howard**
The Viceroy : **John Mills**
Walker : **Martin Sheen**
Kasturba Gandhi : **Rohini Hattangady**
Charlie Andrews : **Ian Charleson**
General Smuts : **Athol Fugard**
Hermann Kallenbach : **Gunther Maria Halmer**
Sardar Patel : **Saeed Jaffrey**
Mirabehn : **Geraldine James**
Mohamed Ali Jinnah : **Alyque Padamsee**
Khan : **Amrish Puri**
Pandit Nehru : **Roshan Seth**
Senior Police Officer : **Ian Bannen**
Principal Secretary : **Michael Bryant**
Advocate General : **John Clements**
Collins : **Richard Griffiths**
Kinnoch : **Nigel Hawthorne**
G.O.C. : **Bernard Hepton**
Sir George Hodge : **Michael Hordern**
Professor Gokhale : **Shreeram Lagoo**
Nahari : **Om Puri**
Maulana Azad : **Virendra Razdan**
Sir Edward Gait : **Richard Vernon**
Nathuram Godse : **Harsh Nayar**
Prakash : **Prabhakar Patankar**
Apte : **Vijay Kashyap**
Karkare : **Nigam Prakash**
Manu : **Supriya Pathak**
Abha : **Nina Gupta**
Commentator : **Shane Rimmer**
Lord Mountbatten : **Peter Harlowe**
J. B. Kripalani : **Anang Desai**
Porter : **Winston Ntshona**
European Passenger : **Peter Cartwright**
Conductor : **Marius Weyers**
Baker : **Richard Mayes**
Tyeb Mohammed : **Alok Nath**
Singh : **Dean Gasper**
Police Sergeant : **Ken Hutchison**
Reporter : **Norman Chancer**
Rich Merchant : **Gulshan Kapoor**
Ayah : **Charu Bala Chokshi**
Harilal Gandhi : **Raj Chaturvedi**
Manilal Gandhi : **Avpar Jhita**
Ramdas Gandhi : **Anthony Sagger**
Daniels : **David Gant**
Colin : **Daniel Day Lewis**
Youths : **Ray Burdis, Daniel Peacock**
Colin's Mother : **Avis Bunnage**
Sonja Schlesin : **Caroline Hutchison**
Tyeb Mohammed's Friend : **Mohan Agashe**
Man In Gallery : **Sudhanshu Mishra**
Miner : **Dina Nath**
Manager of the mine : **John Savident**
Mounted police sergeant : **John Patrick**
Clergyman : **Michael Godley**
Prison officer : **Stewart Harwood**
Prison guard : **Stanley McGeagh**
Young Englishman : **Christopher Good**
Older Englishman : **David Markham**
Young Indian Reporter : **Jyoti Sarup**
English reporter : **John Naylor**

American reporter : **Wilson George**
Older Indian reporter : **Hansu Mehta**
Motilal Nehru : **Sudarshan Sethi**
Mrs Motilal Nehru : **Sunila Pradhan**
Travellers on train roof : **Moti Makan, Jalal Agha**
Cavalry troop leader : **Rupert Frazer**
Shukla : **Manohar Pitale**
Nehru's friends : **Homi Daruvala, K. K. Raina,
    Vivek Swaroop, Raja Biswas**
Subaltern : **Dominic Guard**
Sergeant Putnam : **Bernard Hill**
Village leader : **Rama Kant Jha**
Villager : **Nana Palsikar**
Villager's wife : **Alpna Gupta**
Policeman : **Chandrakant Thakkar**
Batsman : **John Quentin**
Wicket-keeper : **Graham Seed**
Major : **Keith Drinkel**
Police guard : **Bob Barbenia**
Magistrate : **Gerald Sim**
Clerk : **Colin Farrell**
Young Man : **Sanjeev Puri**
Secretary : **Gareth Forwood**
Chauffeur : **Vijay Crishna**
Servant : **Sankalp Dubey**
Brigadier : **James Cossins**
Speaker in Jallianwala Bagh : **Gurcharan Singh**
A.D.C. : **John Vine**
Government Advocate : **Geoffrey Chater**
Lord Hunter : **Ernest Clark**
Indian Barrister : **Habib Tanveer**
Mahadev Desai : **Pankaj Mohan**
Policemen at Chauri Chaura : **Subhash Gupta, Aadil**
Marchers at Chauri Chaura : **Rajeshwar Nath, S. S. Thakur**
Boy with goat : **Rahul Gupta**
Police superintendent : **Barry John**
Clerk of Court : **Brian Oulton**
Court reporters : **James Snell, John Boxer, Gerard Norman**
General Edgar : **Bernard Horsfall**
Brigadier : **Richard Leech**
Pyarelal : **Pankaj Kapoor**
Sarojini Naidu : **Tarla Mehta**
Subaltern : **David Sibley**
Zia : **Daleep Tahil**
Police officer : **Stanley Lebor**
Ramsay MacDonald : **Terrence Hardiman**
Little girl : **Monica Gupta**
Colonel : **Jon Croft**
Adjutant : **William Hoyland**
American lieutenant : **John Ratzenberger**
Major at Aga Khan Palace : **Jack McKenzie**
Doctor at Aga Khan Palace : **Tom Alter**
Lady Mountbatten : **Jane Myerson**
Hindu Youth at ashram : **Roop Kumar Razdan**
Woman refugee : **Bani Sharad Joshi**
Man refugee : **Vagish Kumar Singh**
Abdul Ghaffar Khan : **Dilsher Singh**
Police Commissioner : **Sudheer Dalavi**
Tahib : **Tilak Raj**
Sushila Nayar : **Irpinder Puri**
Hindu youths in Calcutta Street : **Prem Kapoor, Vinay Apte,
    Aswani Kumar, Avinash Dogra, Shreedhar Joshi, Suhas Palshikar**
Nehru's aide : **Karkirat Singh**
Suhrawardy : **Sekhar Chatterjee**
Goondas : **Amarjit, Pratap Desai, Bhatawadekar Prakash, Sunil Shende,
    Rovil Sinha**
Devadas Gandhi : **Amitab Srivastava**

THE PRODUCTION UNIT

PRODUCTION OFFICE

In charge of production : Terence A. Clegg
Associate producer : Suresh Jindal
Production managers : Alexander De Grunwald, Shama Habibullah
Location managers : Graham Ford, Sudesh Syal
Unit managers : Grania O'Shannon, Gerry Levy, Rashid Abbasi
Assistant unit managers : Nasir Abdullah, P. V. Rao
2nd unit production manager : Devi Dutt
2nd unit location manager : Rajiv Suri
Production buyer : Vala Kothari
Transport captain : Brian Hathaway
Transport manager : Major K. N. Sethi

Chief accountant : Pat Howell
Production accountant : Terry Mellis
Assistant accountants : Jo Hannam, E. R. Gopinathan
Production co-ordinator : Loretta Ordewer
Production secretary : Judith Bunn
Delhi liaison : Mohini Banerji
London contact & post-production assistant : Margaret Adams
Producer's secretary : Clare Howard
Production assistants : Sharlene Chatelier, Eleanor Chaudhuri, Dilshad Panday

ON THE SET

First assistant director : David Tomblin
Continuity : June Randall
Assistant to the director : Michael White
Assistant directors : Steve Lanning, Roy Button, Peter Waller, Kamal Swaroop, M. Shahjehan, Bhisham Bhasin, Julian Wall
Standby props : Tony Teiger
Standby rigger : Nobby Clark
Standby painter : Mickey Guyett
Standby plasterer : Joe Lear

Standby carpenter : Jeff Reid
2nd unit first assistant directors : U. S. Pani, John Matthew
2nd unit continuity : Padma Iyer
Stunt co-ordinator : Gerry Crampton
Special effects supervisor : David Watkins
Unit doctor : Dr S. Krishna
Catering : The Location Caterers Ltd.
Catering assistant : G. D. Bakshi

CAMERA

Director of photography : Billy Williams B.S.C.
Director of photography : Ronnie Taylor B.S.C
2nd unit director/cameraman : Govind Nihalani
Camera operator : Chic Anstiss
Focus puller : Ted Deason
Clapper loader : Danny Shelmerdine
Camera grip : Jimmy Waters
Second camera operator : A. K. Bir
Second camera focus puller : Devlin Bose

Second camera assistants : Ashwini Kaul, G. S. Bhasker
2nd unit focus puller : K. Kanti
2nd unit assistant cameraman : Gyan Sahay
2nd unit camera grip : D. Panday
Aerial photographer : Robin Browne
Electrical supervisor : Alan Martin
Best boy : Terry Goddard
Camera maintenance : Nobby Godden

ART DEPARTMENT

Production designer : Stuart Craig
Supervising art director : Bob Laing
Art directors : Ram Yedekar, Norman Dorme
Assistant art directors : Cliff Robinson, Agnes Fernandez
Draughtsman : Roger Cain
Set decorator : Michael Seirton

Set dressers : Jill Quertier, Nissar Allana, Amal Allana, Aruna Harprasad
Construction manager : Dick Frift
Construction liaison : G. Dixit
Property master : Charles Torbett
Main titles : Advance Film Promotions

SOUND

Sound recordist : Simon Kaye
Sound boom operator : Nigel Davis

Sound maintenance : Taffy Haines
Sound assistant : Rajan Rajkhowa

WARDROBE

Costume designers : John Mollo, Bhanu Athaiya
Wardrobe master : Nicholas Ede
Wardrobe mistress : Sally Downing

Indian wardrobe adviser : Sina Kaul
Wardrobe assistants : V. K. Dixit, Shernaz Italia, Aperna Katara, Vinod Kumar, Pavan Malhotra

MAKE-UP AND HAIRDRESSING

Make-up supervisor : Tom Smith
Make-up assistants : John Webber, Connie Reeve, Mustaque Sheikh, Tony Horsfield

Chief hairdresser : Paula Gillespie
Assistant hairdressers : Vera Mitchell, Mariam Samuel

EDITING AND DUBBING

Film editor : John Bloom
Sound editor : Jonathan Bates
Assembly editor : Chris Ridsdale
Associate editor : Alan Patillo

Dubbing mixers : Gerry Humphreys, Robin O'Donoghue
Dialogue editor : Archie Ludski
Assistant editors : Mick Monks, Neil Farrell, Raj Kothari, Gary Beard

MUSIC

Music : Ravi Shankar
Sitar : Ravi Shankar
Assistant conductor & Bānsurī : Vijay Raghav Rao
Voice & tamburā : Lakshmi Shankar
Sārangī : Sultan Khan
Sarod : Ashish Khan
Shahnāī : Sharad Kumar
Voice & santoor & percussion : Ashit Desai
Mrdangam : T. K. Ramakrishnan
Master percussionist : Parasher Desai

Orchestral score & additional music : George Fenton
Conductor : George Fenton
With members of the Wren Orchestra

Music recordist : John Richards
Music co-ordinators : Vijay Raghav Rao, Francis Silkstone

Original soundtrack available on RCA Records

ADVISERS

Historical consultant : Professor R. Puri
Military and police liaison : Air Commodore S. Banerji

Researcher : Lorna Mueller
Military adviser : Colonel Balachandra

PUBLICITY AND CASTING

Director of publicity : Diana Hawkins
Casting director : Susie Figgis
Unit publicity/Indian casting : Dolly Thakore
Assistant : Soonu Ghadially

Publicity secretary : Diana White
Stillsman : Frank Connor
2nd unit stillsman : Pablo Bartholomew
Crowd casting : Yog Batra, Shailendra Goel, Jill Mellis

PRODUCERS, WRITER AND DIRECTOR

Co-producer : Rani Dube
Executive producer : Michael Stanley-Evans
Screenwriter : John Briley
Producer & director : Richard Attenborough

Filmed in Panavision   Processed by Technicolor   Dolby Stereo

Filmed on location in India, the United Kingdom and at Shepperton Studio Centre, England, with post production at
Twickenham Studios, Middlesex, England

THE HINDI VERSION

Lipsynch translators & supervisors : Vinod Sharma, Kamlakar Datey
Consultants : Rani Dube, Roshan Seth
Dubbing editor : Chris Ridsdale
Sound recordist : G. S. Bhatia

Assistant : Jaydev Hattangady
Casting : Dolly Thakore
Producer & director : Richard Attenborough

All the principal artists dubbed their own voices with the exception of the following:

Mahatma Gandhi : Pankaj Kapoor
Margaret Bourke-White : Simi Garewal
General Dyer : Kulbhushan Kharbanda
Lord Irwin : Vinod Sharma
Judge Broomfield : Dinesh Thakur
The Viceroy : Sanjeev Kumar
Walker : Brij Bhushan Sawhney
Charlie Andrews : K. K. Raina
General Smuts : Iftekhar
Hermann Kallenbach : Shekhar Kapoor
Mirabehn : Kavita Chowdhury

Mohamed Ali Jinnah : Manohar Singh
Collins : Jalal Agha
Kinnoch : A. K. Hangal
Sir George Hodge : Arvind Mehra
Sir Edward Gait : Mahesh Sharma
Commentator : Harish Bhimani
Lord Mountbatten : Sudhir Pande
Rich Merchant : Murad
Daniels : Arvind Deshpande
Shukla : Kamlakar Datey
Magistrate : Om Shiv Puri

INDEX

Numbers in italics refer to illustrations
RA = Richard Attenborough